SYMPHONY HALL

The First 100 Years

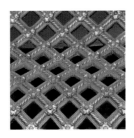

Symphony Hall

The First 100 Years

BOSTON SYMPHONY ORCHESTRA

Symphony Hall: The First 100 Years
ISBN: 0-9671148-2-9

This book was a collaboration between the Boston Symphony Orchestra and Sametz Blackstone Associates.

Boston Symphony Orchestra

Editorial contributors:
Robert Kirzinger
Kim Noltemy-Ugorji
Caroline Smedvig
Mark Volpe
Archival research:
Bridget P. Carr

Sametz Blackstone Associates

Concept, design, editorial contribution, project and production management:
Robert Beerman
Michael Eads
Mark Ledewitz
Roger Sametz

Additional editorial assistance was provided by:
Luise M. Erdmann
Susan Wilson

Symphony Hall: The First 100 Years was printed and bound by Allied Printing Services under the direction of Mark Carter; Bob Zacharie was project manager. Due to the delicate nature of the more than two hundred archival items presented in the book, these items were digitally captured at Allied Printing's digital photography studio.

Production of this book was made possible, in part, by generous contributions from Sametz Blackstone Associates, Boston, and Allied Printing Services, Manchester, Connecticut.

Most of the archival photography and imagery included in this book is from the archives of the Boston Symphony Orchestra. Additional archival imagery courtesy of:

The Bostonian Society: pages 20, 21

The Boston Public Library, Print Department: pages 20, 21, 22, 34, 56, 60, 61, 62, 105, 113

The Boston Public Library, Music Department, Allen A. Brown Collection: page 19

FleetBoston Celebrity Series: page 60

The Handel & Haydn Society: page 14

Isabella Stewart Gardner Museum: page 20

Stadtgeschichtliches Museum Leipzig (Leipzig City Historical Museum): page 32

The Society for the Preservation of New England Antiquities: pages 12, 20, 21, 31

Contemporary photography by:

Roger Farrington: page 60
Charles Gauthier: pages 98, 99, 107
Michael Lutch: pages 101, 112
Constantine Manos: pages 2, 55, 76-93, 116, 117
Stu Rosner: page 107
Len Rubenstein: page 69
Lincoln Russell: back cover
Peter Vanderwarker: front cover, pages 3, 9, 29, 39, 41, 42, 43, 48, 49, 51, 95, 115, 119
Miro Vintoniv: pages 64, 67, 94, 107

Original McKim, Mead & White architectural drawings of Symphony Hall courtesy of the New-York Historical Society

Architectural elevations, page 38, courtesy Douglas Yeo

Sabine's papers reprinted from: "Architectural Acoustics: Part I – Reverberation: Calculation in Advance of Construction," *The American Architect and Building News*, v. 68, no. 1277, June 16, 1900

Aaron Copland's introduction to *Portrait of a Symphony* is reprinted by permission of the Aaron Copland Fund for Music, Inc.

INTRODUCTION

Boston is a singular place, a city where art and artists matter, a city where the cabbies are as likely to greet Seiji Ozawa by name as they would Pedro Martinez or Drew Bledsoe.

I can't imagine Boston without Symphony Hall. Though it is now well woven into the center of Boston's cityscape, it's hard to remember that Major Higginson's decision to locate the home of the Boston Symphony at the intersection of Massachusetts and Huntington Avenues was a daring one. In 1900, this location was "The Wild, Wild West," the very fringe of Boston. (Being the Yankee that he was, the bargain price of the land also appealed to him.) The building itself is Bostonian to the core, so much so that Charles Follen McKim must have despaired as he saw his design stripped of much of the ornamentation he had lavished on it. As Robert Campbell points out, Symphony Hall is akin to those Boston ladies who "hid their new gowns from Paris in the closet for a year, so they wouldn't look too fashionable." No Parisian confections here. This is Boston, this is serious—"the real thing," as columnist R. W. Apple puts it.

Symphony Hall is a rare and incalculably refined instrument unto itself. As Leo Beranek explains, the hall's legendary acoustics were not luck, but rather the result of the application of an acoustical formula invented by the young Harvard professor, Wallace Clement Sabine, just prior to the hall's construction. Again, McKim came up against Boston's priorities: His desire for a building entirely unique to New England that would replicate the Greek theater at Epidaurus was rejected in favor of a more prosaic design, but one proven more hospitable to acoustics. I am convinced that the magnificence of the Boston Symphony sound is inextricably linked to the orchestra's having grown up in this miraculous hall. Here, musicians never have to force sound from that stage. It fills the hall in an almost effortless way.

From the beginning, Symphony Hall has always been a good citizen, a musical meeting-house of the New England tradition. In addition to providing a home for the BSO, the Handel & Haydn Society and countless performers of all stripes, its doors were open to the community in myriad ways, from the more whimsical and frivolous occasional automobile and power boat show to a Communist Party meeting (in the 1930s).

I love this hall. I love the beauty in its understatement; its grace and mystery, its awe-inspiring past. If architecture is frozen music, as Goethe said, it seems that the reverberations of thousands of performances have been absorbed by the walls, reinforcing the very foundation of Symphony Hall and rendering it an even more hallowed space today than at its inception.

I invite you to join me in reading this celebration of our dear and cherished building, to learn its secrets, to understand its lore, and to appreciate the hold it has on performer and listener alike. ❧

—*Yo-Yo Ma*

Portrait of Henry Lee Higginson (1834-1919), founder of the Boston Symphony Orchestra and benefactor of Symphony Hall, as photographed by William Notman

As the century turned: Boston in 1900

On October 15, 1900, Symphony Hall made its debut, and a finer reception could not have been imagined. Boston's newspapers reveled in the acoustic excellence and architectural beauty of "Boston's Temple of Music" and the "City's New Glory." The Boston Symphony Orchestra's rendering of Beethoven's *Missa Solemnis* was praised as "the most successful performance of [the piece] that has ever been given in America."

The wit, wisdom, and wealth of the city, represented by Emersons, Cabots, Winthrops, Longfellows, Hemingways, and Gardners, packed the hall. "Society and Talent Worship at Music's Shrine," noted one bemused journalist; another admitted, "If one wished to tell who were present at the opening of the new music hall this evening, he would have to transcribe a large portion of Boston society's blue book."

From the beginning, however, the hall was not the exclusive province of the socially prominent: "For years Boston's music lovers—and their name is legion—have patiently looked forward to and waited and hoped for a new home," explained a reporter for the *Boston Herald*. "No more brilliant or important event has ever figured in the musical history of Boston.... In fact," the writer added, "*everybody* was pleased."

In one sense, the opening of Symphony Hall at the turn of the twentieth century was the fulfillment of one man's dream. Henry Lee Higginson, a prominent businessman and philanthropist, had founded Boston's symphony orchestra in 1881. Less than two decades later, he personally financed an elegant new home for his beloved musicians.

In many ways, the hall's opening was a great historic and cultural landmark as well.

Symphony Hall, c. 1930, before the underpass on Huntington Avenue was built

It was, in essence, the culmination of decades of growth—economic, social, political, architectural, topographical, and cultural—in the life of Boston, the self-avowed Athens of America.

THE PILGRIMS' PROGRESS

Boston was founded in 1630 by Englishman John Winthrop and the Puritans of the Massachusetts Bay Colony. It began as a 780-acre, pear-shaped peninsula called Shawmut—roughly translated as "land of the living waters"—by its native inhabitants. In the colonial and early national period, the town thrived on successful fishing, shipbuilding, and sailing industries; with time, an international sea trade was established, creating fortunes for both shipowners and importers, who became Boston's maritime merchant-princes.

In its musical life, early Boston was predictably Puritan. The singing of psalms was accepted and encouraged, as was attending sermons and lectures. Among the acts strictly forbidden by the colony's religious leaders were making merry music, playing musical instruments in church, dancing, celebrating Christmas, and presenting drama. The Massachusetts General Court saw stage plays as "tending to increase immorality, impiety and a contempt of religion." As a result, no theaters were built in Boston until 1794, and no true concert halls until 1852.

By the end of the nineteenth century, Boston and its inhabitants had changed dramatically. Congregational churches, the direct descendants of Puritan meetinghouses, no longer dominated the religious life of the city. Waves of immigrants filled Boston's neighborhoods with new faces, new accents, and a new labor force. These newcomers did not find acceptance and integration, especially

This October 16, 1900, illustration accompanied the Boston Globe's *review of the inaugural concert in Symphony Hall.*

ON GLOBE, TUESDAY, OCTOBER 16, 1900.

OPENING OF BOSTON'S BEAUTIFUL SYMPHONY HALL.

Exceedingly Large and Refined Audience Enjoys the Initial Performance Under the Direction of Wilhelm Gericke.

WILHELM GERICKE CONDUCTOR.

BOSTON'S NEW TEMPLE OF MUSIC.

NEW HALL FOR MUSIC.

Symphony Concerts in Back Bay.

Description of the Auditorium.

Dedication to Be on Oct. 15.

SYMPHONY HALL.

"Stop at Symphony Hall, please," he said to the conductor of the Huntington Avenue car last evening.

"Never heard of it, sir," replied the conductor.

"Why, that is the name of the new Music Hall, corner of Massachusetts Avenue and Huntington Avenue," spoke up Mr. Fred. Comee, so long connected with the old Music Hall, and who is now at the new temple of music on the Back Bay.

"Oh, yes; I know where that is," said the conductor quickly.

It is a fact that not only the conductors on the street cars, but the public generally, are as yet unfamiliar with the name "Symphony Hall." In recognition of this fact the management of the Boston Elevated Street Railway Company has been requested by the Symphony Hall authorities to instruct its conductors to call out the name of the hall, Monday, when the auction sale of the Symphony Concert tickets begins, as well as on the subsequent days of the sale. Music lovers of Boston, as well as most other people, will soon be as familiar with the location of Symphony Hall as they have long been with the historic old auditorium down town where the world-famous Symphony Concerts were so long held.

Cheerfulness and warmth of color effects were the most dominant characteristics of the hall to the Journal reporter who entered the auditorium about 8 o'clock last evening.

The walls and ceiling are a very light gray in color, and the general plan of interior decoration being of the style of the Italian renaissance. There are two balconies, the seats in both all commanding a fine view of the stage.

All of the seats in the hall are upholstered in rich, dark green leather. They are about the same pattern as those in the old Music Hall, and are all alike. The seating capacity of the hall is 2569. Of this number 466 seats are on the floor, 598 in the first balcony and 505 in the second balcony. This seating capacity of the old Music Hall was 2307. Some of the best seats in the house are those in the upper balcony which Maj. Higginson has decided shall be sold for 25 cents apiece for the Friday afternoon rehearsals. The custom maintained at the old hall is thus continued.

Imposing Proscenium Arch.

The proscenium arch is, perhaps, the most imposing feature of the hall. It is square, and 62 feet by 45 feet in dimensions. A broad band of gold comprises the frame in which is worked a handsome design consisting of acanthus leaves and fruits. On a wide golden scroll, where the keystone of the arch would naturally be, is the name of Beethoven.

A fine organ takes up the entire background of the stage. The decoration of this, as well as the walls of the stage, is in light gray, while the pipes are of gold. There are entrances to the stage at the right and left, through which the musicians can enter and retire.

The organ contains 58 stops; 21 combinations; 10 couplers; 3485 pipes. The console is movable and is attached to the organ by a flexible cable 100 feet in length. The cable contains 372 wires. In the pedal organ there is an open diapason of 32 feet pitch, the longest pipe being large enough for a man to crawl through, turn around, and come out again.

Like the proscenium arch, the balcony railings are of gold color and quite showy. The tops of the balcony rails are upholstered in crimson plush.

Well-Lighted Auditorium.

From the handsomely designed ceiling, done in panels with curved beams, are suspended a number of artistic chandeliers of bronze or brass, which contain hundreds of incandescent lights, of 16 and 32 candle power respectively. These chandeliers are placed so near the ceiling that they will not annoy the audience with their glare. The lights on the stage are placed behind the proscenium arch and are thus out of sight of the people for the most part. Upon the front of the organ are two small clusters of electric lights, too. The lighting arrangements are perfect. There are 2000 electric lamps in all.

The acoustic properties of the hall have not yet been thoroughly tested. Special attention has been given to the matter, however, and an expert on such matters, Prof. Wallace C. Sabine of Harvard University has been employed to make the hall as nearly perfect as possible in this respect.

Last evening Mr. Comee stood upon the stage and talked, in an ordinary tone of voice, with a gentleman seated in the upper balcony. Both could distinguish what the other said without the least trouble. Several selections were also played upon the organ, and this, too, indicated that the acoustic properties of the hall were excellent.

The general public will have a chance to judge for themselves on the night of Monday, Oct. 15, when the first concert to be held in the hall—the dedicatory concert—will be held. On that night Beethoven's mass in D will be given by the full Symphony Orchestra, under Mr. Gericke, with a chorus from the Cecelia Society of 200 voices and a quartet composed of Clementine Devere, Gertrude Mayster, Evan Williams and Joseph Beresheim.

Fireproof Throughout.

Throughout, the building is fireproof, and there are 16 exits from each balcony and from the floor, while the corridors are large enough to hold the entire audience comfortably. On the second floor is a large foyer, or promenade, with an arched ceiling and a gem of an echo. This is on the Huntington Avenue side, right over the main entrance.

There are four coat rooms, two on the floor and two in the first balcony, with a capacity of nearly 2000 boxes. There are also spacious toilet and dressing rooms for ladies and for gentlemen.

A feature of the new hall that will be appreciated is the almost perfect system of heating and ventilation. It is a system said to be in use nowhere else in the world. The cool, fresh air is drawn in from the top of the building, and by means of fans and suction is made to pass through pipes, by which it can be fixed at any temperature, hot or cold, and then is forced into the auditorium from perforations in the ceiling and out again through registers in the floor. In this way, it is claimed that the air will be kept constantly cool and fresh.

The rise in the floor of the auditorium begins at the letter K, and extends to the back wall of the hall; rises also in both balconies, both in the centre and on the sides.

Handsome Entrances and Exits.

There is a marquise over the Massachusetts Avenue entrance, 65 fet in length, which is for the convenience of carriages principally. There will also be ticket offices located at this entrance. The main entrance, however, is on Huntington Avenue.

The exterior of the building suggests the architecture of the North Italian Renaissance. It is very plain, but substantial looking. Ground was broken June 12, 1899. The builders were the Norcross Bros.; the architects, McKim, Mead & White, and the heating and ventilating apparatus was put in under the direction of Alfred R. Wolff, heating expert of New York.

In one of the niches in the rear wall, just above the upper balcony, is a statue of Apollo, exactly like the one that used to grace the rear wall of the old Music Hall.

Mr. Mudgett and Mr. Ellis, as well as Mr. Comee, are delighted with the new hall. They all were on hand last evening to show the representatives of the several newspapers over the building, and pointed out its several beauties and advantages with considerable pride. Mr. Thomas A. Fox, the Boston representative of the architects, was also one of the party.

A description in the Boston Globe *of the architecture and decorative aspects of Boston's "new" music hall three weeks before the opening*

the Irish Catholics, who began arriving in Boston in the mid-nineteenth century, or the Jews and Italians who followed.

Meanwhile, mercantile interests had given way to the world of finance, and Boston's wealthiest, most powerful families had become entrepreneurs and financiers. State Street—once the location of the colonists' "First Church"—had evolved into Boston's financial center, a symbol of its wealth and power. In 1798, Boston had two banks. In 1906, the city had twenty-seven national banks, nineteen trust companies, and money to burn.

Throughout industrial America, the Gay Nineties were in full swing. Despite the market crash of 1893—which hit the South and West harder than it did New York and Boston—self-made millionaires, such as Vanderbilt, Rockefeller, and Carnegie, were living on lavish fortunes made in railroads, steel, oil, financing, and related enterprises. Boston's capitalists owned and directed railroads, and developed copper mines, cotton mills, real estate, lumber, and electricity across the nation.

As might be expected, the desire for culture followed closely on such financial success. Throughout the mid and late 1800s, extended sojourns abroad—for pleasure, study, and work—had become *de rigueur* for wealthy Bostonians, as had emulation of European fads, fashions, art, and architecture. It was only logical, then, that members of this privileged class would bring the best of Europe home to Boston. Many of their purchases were for private pleasure. But these new capitalists, entrepreneurs, and financiers also began creating and maintaining such cultural institutions as the Boston Athenaeum, the Boston Public Library (the country's first major free public library), the Massachusetts Horticultural Society, the Museum of Natural History, and the Boston Museum of Fine Arts.

William Tudor, a founding member of the Boston Athenaeum and editor of the fledgling *North American Review*, was the first to call Boston "the Athens of America," in 1819. By the last quarter of the century, decades of hard work, great talent, and generous patronage had made the name ring true.

The stage was set for Henry Lee Higginson.

THE MAN

Though born in New York, Henry Lee Higginson (1834-1919) was of old New England stock rooted in nine generations of Massachusetts soil, and hailing from a socially and intellectually distinguished family. His father, in Henry's words, "worked pretty hard, [and] passed much of his time and any spare pennies possible in charitable work." Personal industriousness and a charitable bent were also the son's destiny. Once his family moved back to Boston, young Henry was expected to attend Boston Latin School and Harvard College. His classmates in the Harvard Class of 1855 included Phillips Brooks and Alexander Agassiz. He also befriended a group of students from fine old Boston clans—including Robert Gould Shaw, Charles Russell Lowell, and Stephen George Perkins—who were later slain in the Civil War. A series of eye problems excused Higginson from his Harvard studies, freeing him to travel to Germany and Austria to pursue his passion for music.

Higginson remembered his early enchantment with the musical world in an address to members of the Boston Symphony Orchestra in 1914:

Sixty years ago I wished to be a musician, and therefore went to Vienna, where I studied two years and a half diligently, learned something of music, something about musicians, and one other thing—that I had no talent for music.

If his skill on the piano was limited, his appreciation of good music knew no bounds. Though it would take years to bear fruit, Higginson's youthful notion that the wonderful orchestras he had heard in Vienna should be replicated in Boston would eventually become a reality.

In 1863, Higginson was betrothed to Ida Agassiz, the daughter of Louis Agassiz, Harvard's most famous professor, and Elizabeth Cary Agassiz, a founder and the first president of Radcliffe College. But their life together was interrupted by the Civil War—and the mission to end the slavery that Higginson so abhorred—which proved a privilege to serve and a heartbreak to endure. Commissioned as a second lieutenant in 1861, Higginson was eventually promoted to first lieutenant, then captain, then major. After surviving three saber cuts and two pistol shots in the Battle of Aldie, he was discharged for disability in August 1864. (The saber cut on his cheek was not, as many assume, a war wound but the result of a private scuffle over a horse.) Major Higginson—

"The Great Organ" in the "old" Boston Music Hall; it was removed in the 1880s, and, after years of disuse, was finally moved to the Methuen Memorial Music Hall in 1909.

as he was known for the rest of his life—could legitimately have been called "Colonel," his rank when discharged; but that name was reserved for his older cousin, Thomas Wentworth Higginson, an abolitionist, writer, war veteran, and correspondent of Emily Dickinson's.

After his war service, Henry Lee Higginson began searching for a career. By 1865, he was working in Ohio, unsuccessfully developing oil wells; he then suffered another failure in the world of cotton. On January 1, 1868, however, he became a partner in the Boston banking firm of Lee, Higginson & Company—begun in 1848 by John C. Lee of Salem and George Higginson of Boston—where he remained until his death, more than half a century later.

Lee, Higginson & Company was a well-respected, stalwart, and eminently conservative backbone of State Street. Their success and fame came from financing ventures that helped develop the Calumet copper mines; the Bell Telephone Company; the Atcheson, Topeka, Santa Fe, and Union Pacific railroads; the Walter Baker Chocolate Company; and the companies which became General Electric, among many others.

Higginson later mused, in a 1908 letter, that he was not really wanted in his family's successful State Street firm: "I was taken in at the beginning of 1868 as a matter of charity, to keep me out of the poorhouse." As author Bliss Perry noted in his *Life and Letters of Henry Lee Higginson* (1921), Higginson and State Street were an odd, though lucrative, coupling:

He had come to anchor on State Street. Certainly it was not the port he had first looked for, and some of his lifelong intimates… persisted in thinking him temperamentally out of tune with his calling. He once said… that he never walked into 44 State Street without wanting to sit down on the doorstep and cry….

It is not recorded that this lover of music ever did sit down and weep…. What is certain is … it was State Street … that gave him opportunity to render an unmatched service to the community.

All good work takes time and life-blood—and shows us why most of us must live long to do a real piece of work. —Henry Lee Higginson, July 21, 1887

By the time Major Higginson was financially prepared to endow Boston with a symphony orchestra and a hall, the city was ready to accept his gifts. Perhaps most important, musical taste and a taste for music had grown significantly since the days of Puritan psalmody.

The first glimmer of hope that serious and orchestral music could find an audience in Boston had actually appeared in Puritan days. The city's religious fathers placed harsh restrictions on colonial festivities, part of a grand plan to "purify" the tainted ways of the Church of England. Ironically, they also enticed more than one colonial youth into forbidden places like the Anglican King's Chapel, on the corner of Tremont and School streets. Here, amid a congregation of British citizens and their Loyalist friends, colonists could attend Christmas pageants and hear the first organ permanently installed in a church in British North America (1713-14).

A pivotal event in the development of a modern music sensibility in Boston—and the first important organization of music lovers—was the Peace Jubilee held at King's Chapel at the end of the War of 1812. The choruses assembled to sing selections from Handel's *Messiah* and Haydn's *The Creation* became, in time, the Handel & Haydn Society (1815). Then, in 1833, the Boston Academy of Music was formed. Though its purpose was education, it produced a series of concerts in 1840-41, considered milestones in the city's music history; it was in these programs that Beethoven was

The Handel & Haydn Society, 1914, onstage in Symphony Hall, with Emil Mollenhauer, conductor, and H. G. Tucker, organist

reportedly first heard in Boston. Moreover, the Harvard Music Association had been founded in 1837; it was an influential club inspired and dominated by John Sullivan Dwight, the dean of musical taste and opinion in Boston in the middle to late 1800s.

By mid-century, more and more concerts took place in Boston, including those by the touring Germania Musical Society and by the Philharmonic Society, begun by Carl Zerrahn in 1857. But even when serious performances of orchestral music were scarce, musical study, discussion, and writing abounded. Magazines that centered on, or included, articles about music proliferated throughout the nineteenth century. The first issue of the *Dial* (1840), for example, included an article by John Sullivan Dwight, who dreamed of "an orchestra worthy to execute the grand works of Haydn and Mozart."

In the 1840s, the New England philosophy known as transcendentalism was gathering strength. So too were its brilliant literary exponents, including Ralph Waldo Emerson, Margaret Fuller, Bronson Alcott, and Henry David Thoreau. Many of these writers were sometime residents of Brook Farm, a communal living experiment in West Roxbury. And many of them loved analyzing music. When Dwight wrote his article for the *Dial*, he was, in the words of the author Mark DeWolfe Howe, "soon to become a Brook Farmer, and long to remain the chief apostle of music in Boston." Moreover, Dwight became a regular music reviewer for a variety of local papers while producing his own *Journal of Music* from 1852 to 1881.

Dwight, the Harvard Music Association, and their friends all helped to lobby for a performance space in the city built specifically for musical productions. The Boston Music Hall opened to great fanfare in 1852. It was on Hamilton Place, near today's Park Street subway stop on Tremont Street, and its remnants were incorporated into the Orpheum Theater, which stands in its place today. It was here that popular vocalists like Jenny Lind, "the Swedish Nightingale," could perform on a real stage rather than in makeshift venues. (Often quoted is Mark DeWolfe Howe's wry observation: "The Music Hall was built in 1852, from which time forward it was unnecessary to ask a visiting Jenny Lind to sing in the Fitchburg Railroad Station.") Here, too, visiting orchestras from Europe could whet the musical appetites of their increasingly large Boston audiences.

For many years I had hard work to earn my living and support my wife.... All these years I watched the musical conditions in Boston, hoping to make them better. I believed that an orchestra of excellent musicians under one head and devoted to a single purpose could produce fine results, and wished for the ability to support such an undertaking. —Henry Lee Higginson, April 27, 1914

In 1881, Major Higginson established Boston's first, full-size symphony orchestra, which used the Boston Music Hall as its home and primary performance space. More than a decade later, when the Music Hall was threatened with demolition due to downtown construction, Higginson decided to build a brand-new hall for his Boston Symphony Orchestra in a recently developed section of town.

Years afterward, Charles W. Eliot—longtime Harvard president and Higginson friend—thanked Major Higginson for his gift:

Boston was historically the right place in the United States to develop an orchestra of high merit. The soil in which you planted the Boston Symphony Orchestra [and Symphony Hall]... had been well prepared during the forty years preceding by a series of earlier organizations... in the

The Germania Musical Society, an orchestra of young musicians from Berlin, who performed in Boston in the mid-1800s

community where you and I grew up....Their resources were limited, and their achievements modest; but they made ready a supporting public for you.

President Eliot had more to be thankful for than most. At the same time that Higginson was supporting the symphony and its hall, he was also supporting Harvard. The deaths of several of his closest friends in the Civil War inspired him to make a generous gift to that institution: Soldiers Field, where Harvard Stadium stands today, was donated in 1890 by Higginson as a memorial to fallen alumni. Elected a member of the Harvard Corporation in 1893, the Major made a number of other large donations to the university, including $150,000 for the construction of the Harvard Union (now the Barker Center).

THE LAND

It was more than just the music-loving public that was ready to embrace Henry Lee Higginson at the turn of the twentieth century. When Higginson built Symphony Hall on the corner of Huntington and Massachusetts avenues in 1900, he was also contributing to a long progression of physical growth in Boston, which had changed from a town to a city in 1822. The land itself had grown—from a scrawny peninsula of 780 acres to a sprawling metropolis of 24,610 acres by century's end. Part of that growth came from the acquisition of outlying districts and communities between 1804 and 1912. The rest was man-made—a series of ambitious landfill, beautification, and building projects that included the tidal Back Bay and a marshy wasteland called the Fens.

Since the end of the Civil War, urban dwellers had grown from 16 to 30 percent of America's population. Immigration had swelled these ranks further, adding to the overcrowding in major cities. Unlike New York and Philadelphia, however, Boston dealt with this problem by acquiring and creating new land, then connecting it all by public transportation systems. Boston's elite had always enjoyed traveling to lovely neighborhoods outside Boston proper, where they built fashionable country estates. But the addition of horsecars (1856), electrified trolleys (1889), and America's first subway (1897) made Boston's "streetcar suburbs" accessible to all classes of people.

Another innovation that linked the old Boston and the new was the Emerald Necklace of Boston parks. During the last two decades of the nineteenth century, Frederick Law Olmsted—the acknowledged Father of Landscape Architecture, who designed Manhattan's Central Park with

R.W. Apple
The Real Thing

I am ill-placed to celebrate the glories of Symphony Hall, since I am neither a musician nor a Boston Symphony Orchestra subscriber—nor, indeed, a Bostonian. But these handicaps in no way enfeeble the emotions I feel about that grand old building on Huntington Avenue, where I have thrilled to so much magnificent music under the leadership of Koussevitzky, Munch, Steinberg, and now Ozawa. The Musikverein in Vienna is extra-ordinary, especially on New Year's Day. Finlandia Hall in Helsinki, which proves that great modern design and good acoustics need not be mortal enemies, has its own special appeal. Severance Hall in Cleveland, recently restored, retains its hometown hold on me. But Symphony Hall remains unique, watched over by the spirit of that remarkable Brahmin, Henry Lee Higginson.

It was a much-loved great-aunt, Marguerite Barton, who introduced me to Boston itself at a very young age, and she took me to Symphony Hall for the first time when I was about ten. Having grown up near Cleveland, I already knew George Szell and Severance Hall—not exactly bush-leaguers. But something about Symphony Hall—its sonic splendor, certainly, but also its New England propriety and reserve—won me over, instantly and permanently. I have visited it for more than fifty years now, man and boy, as a student, as an itinerant political reporter, as a stepfather entertaining offspring studying at Harvard, and it has never lost its capacity to thrill me and put me on my mettle.

"Concentrate!" those old walls whisper. "This is the real thing."

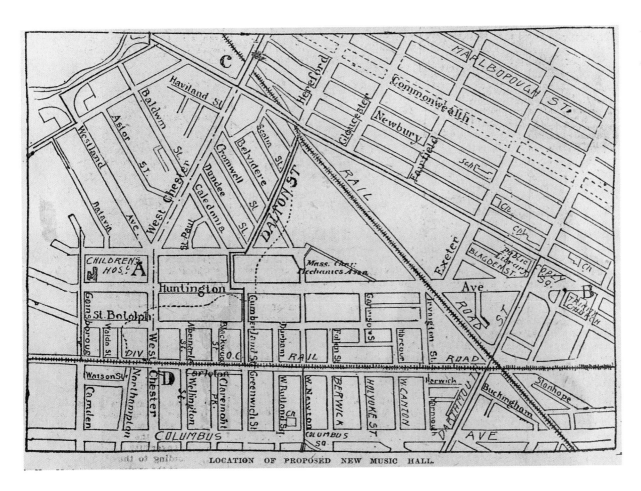

A map of Boston's Back Bay in the late 1800s; "A" marks the site proposed for Symphony Hall.

Calvert Vaux in 1857—was hired to design, develop, and improve a series of public parklands in Boston, from Boston Common and the Public Garden through the new contours of the Back Bay Fens and out to Franklin Park. Like the public transportation system, these parks were open to all.

It is no coincidence that Olmsted's development of green space was paralleled by massive building projects throughout Boston. As the new century approached, bold new buildings were constructed all over town. The granite Ames Mercantile Building became the city's first skyscraper in 1888. The Custom House tower, added to the old Custom House in 1913, became the city's tallest structure—an honor it maintained until the Prudential Center was built in 1965. Though height restrictions prevented Boston's becoming a city of dark canyons like Manhattan, turn-of-the-century newspaper headlines continually heralded the skyscrapers' coming of age in Boston, not to mention their profitability.

Meanwhile, to the west of the old downtown, the Back Bay was changing the city's shape and content. In the middle of the nineteenth century, the city's Back Bay was exactly that—the mud-flat backside of Boston, which flooded when Atlantic tides swelled the lower reaches of the Charles River. Between 1857 and 1890, however, this unsightly, foul-smelling area underwent a mammoth landfill project that transformed it into high-priced land and exclusive addresses. With Commonwealth Avenue and its mall as a backbone, prominent architect Arthur Gilman designed the area in the grid pattern then popular in France's Second Empire. Long boulevards and avenues were regularly intersected by a series of streets named in alphabetical order. Huntington Avenue, which veered off from the grid on a diagonal, was laid out in 1872.

The developers and builders immediately followed, and much of the land was sold on the open market for cash. Among the first buyers was David Stewart, a wealthy New Yorker who built a home for his daughter at 152 Beacon Street; Isabella Stewart Gardner lived here until the end of

BOSTON'S HANDSOME NEW MUSIC HALL.

Beautiful Classical Building That Is Planned for the Corner of Huntington and Massachusetts Avenues.

THE PROPOSED NEW MUSIC HALL.

The above drawing is that of the proposed new Music Hall, which is to be located at Huntington and Massachusetts avenues. The building, as can be seen from the picture, is one of the finest and handsomest yet designed for this city. The cut is from a water-color perspective.

McKim, Mead & White, the New York architects, are the designers of the building, and a representative of theirs came on with the plans yesterday morning. He later superintended the hanging of these drawings on the walls of the offices in the Tremont building. The plans will be at the offices for a week, where they can be viewed by the stockholders of the company which is to build and own the building.

The material to be used is red brick and stone. The main entrance, which will be on Huntington avenue, will be very graceful and of unique design. The portico will be Ionic, and eight stone pillars will produce a very artistic as well as grand effect. The central hall occupies the main part of the building, and it rises to a height of three stories. The wings of the building on either side of this hall are to be built to the height of two stories only. There are to be slight inclines running from the roofs of the wings to the roof of the main hall. This will give the building the effect of having two stories with an enlarged monitor roof in the middle, which runs the entire length of the structure.

This plan was adopted so that the entire interior of the central part of the building is made the music hall, while the side structures include the entrances, lobbies, side corridors and business offices. The latter are on the different floors, but they allow of a deeper gallery space.

By a careful examination of the drawing, one can appreciate what the architects propose to do in giving to Boston a beautiful and finely equipped building to be used solely for musical entertainments. The hall has been designed primarily with a view to providing an edi-

fice for the concerts of the Symphony orchestra, the Handel and Haydn Society, and kindred organizations. It is in no sense adapted to the uses of an opera house.

But for all that, one important fact has not been forgotten. The architect had in view the possibility of there being a demand in this new building for a number of banquets, and he has accordingly provided for such a want. His plans call for a kitchen in the basement, and a serving room on the hall floor beyond the south corridor.

The building is very classic in style, although it is not patterned after any edifice elsewhere. The report has been current that the architects have used ideas in accordance with those of an opera house in Munich. This they say is not so; that the building is entirely original in its conception.

The one who looks at the water-color representation of this building is at once impressed with its beauty and simplicity of design. Over the entrance on Huntington avenue is the inscription, "Boston Music Hall." Above this in the main front wall is a place for a tablet, for whatever inscription may be thought best. On either side of the portico are two indentations, one in the front wall and another in the side, just around the corner of the building. The idea of the architects in providing these niches was to make places for statuary. There are seven doors leading to the broad vestibule, which runs the entire length of the building. Beyond the vestibule is the lobby, while the ticket office is in the centre of the wall which divides the vestibule and the lobby.

Two corridors, 14 feet wide, extend along the side of the hall the entire length, in much the same manner as do those in the old hall. Doors enter from the corridors at frequent intervals, the hall being entirely inclosed except for these openings. Another entrance, which is by way of Massachusetts avenue, will be that for the carriages. It is in about the centre of the building, and it opens into a small vestibule. A marquee is provided at this doorway.

The hall itself is 140 feet long and 75 feet wide. The open stage is in the rear—that is, when entrance is made from the front lobby. There are four aisles passing through the hall, two in the middle and one on each side. While

the seats are at an incline, the slope is not so great as in a theatre, but just enough to allow those who sit in the rear seats to have full command of the stage.

Light is let into the hall by windows in the front and rear of the main structure. The windows are large arched affairs of stained glass, these arches extending almost from the roof line of the side structures to the ceiling of the music hall. It is also planned that niches be placed in the walls between the windows, as places for statuary. This is only one of the many plans which have been proposed for the general scheme of interior decorations.

The first of the two galleries extends along the side limits of the hall, and is set into the side structures for a short distance. Except for a slight curvature in the rear, the side lines of the balconies are straight. This furnishes a narrow side balcony with a broad rear. While the second balcony is much the same as the first, it is not so broad in the rear, and does not extend beyond the hall space on the sides. On the first balcony there is a vestibule in the rear and corridors along the side, the same as on the floor. The second balcony has a lobby and a corridor on either side.

The exact seating capacity will be 2630. This is a gain over the old hall of 233. The floor capacity will be 1511, that of the first balcony 608 and of the second 511. The seats are to be larger and more comfortable than those in the old hall. While the old hall had three rows of seats in the first balcony, the new one will have but two.

Much care has been taken for the prevention of draughts. It is proposed to close the two inner doors leading to the auditorium, and to have the people enter by the right and left through doors which will be sufficiently large. While in the old hall two sections of seats on the first balcony overlooked the stage, not a seat in all the new hall will be over the stage.

The various needs of the orchestra and choral societies which have occasion to use the hall will be met by the use of the side rooms, which are to be in the two-story part of the building. On each of the four corners there is a staircase in the side sections, furnishing ample ways for coming into or going out of the building. For this reason the side sections are carried to sufficient height so

that they contain the stairways to the second gallery.

The offices of the managers of the hall and the Symphony orchestra are on the side of the Massachusetts avenue section. The ladies' reception room is at the east end of this entrance and is very elaborate in its appointments, and has a toilet room adjoining. There is also a toilet room for men. An "artist's room," as it is called, has been reserved on the Massachusetts avenue side of the stage. The corresponding room on the other side of the stage is to be used as a tuning room for the members of the orchestra.

On the first gallery there are additional cloak and toilet rooms. On the Massachusetts avenue side two large rooms have been set off for libraries of the Symphony orchestra and the Handel and Haydn Society. There is still another room for artists on this floor, while two more have not yet been assigned. On the same floor, is a room 34x37, designated for a chorus room. It is to be used for rehearsals of choruses or smaller orchestras, or, in fact, for any similar purpose. There are ventilating shafts on either side of the stage.

These plans have only been submitted to the Music Hall stockholders for their consideration, and have as yet not been accepted. The representative of the architects who brought them here yesterday said that it would be impossible to make any estimate on how much it would cost to construct such a building, as it depended greatly on many details.

GRAND ARMY LEADERSHIP.

Senior Vice-Commander Johnson Will Be a Candidate.

CINCINNATI, O., March 13, 1899. , W. C. Johnson, senior vice-commander-in-chief of the Grand Army of the Republic, today issued a call for the executive committee of the national board of administration of the Grand Army to meet in Philadelphia on April 12 to select a commander-in-chief to succeed the late Gen. James A. Sexton.

Senior Vice-Commander Johnson has been indorsed by the department of Ohio, and will be a candidate for the leadership.

the 1900s. (She then moved farther west—to the reclaimed marshlands called the Fens, where her namesake museum remains to this day.) Her good friend Henry Lee Higginson also lived in the Back Bay, first at the Hotel Hamilton (1870) on Clarendon Street, then in a house at 191 Commonwealth Avenue (1874).

Cultural and educational institutions immediately flocked to and flourished in the new Back Bay. The Commonwealth donated large parcels of land to worthy entities such as the Massachusetts Institute of Technology, the Boston Society of Natural History, the Massachusetts Normal Art School, Trinity Church, and the City of Boston. Meanwhile, many churches from older, more congested sections of town also saw opportunities for grand new buildings, designed by some of the city's finest architects. The illustrious Henry Hobson Richardson created both the stunning Trinity Church (1877) in Copley Square and the Brattle Street Church's new home (1871) at Commonwealth Avenue and Clarendon Street. Arthur Gilman designed the Arlington Street Church (1859), and Richard Upjohn drew up plans for the Central Congregational Church (1867), at Newbury and Berkeley streets.

COPLEY SQUARE AND THE CULTURAL MILE

The area once known as Art Square—renamed Copley in 1883, to honor Boston-born portrait painter John Singleton Copley—was a perfect symbol of the Back Bay's greatest aspirations by the end of the nineteenth century. On the site of today's Fairmont Copley Plaza Hotel was the Museum of Fine Arts (1876); diagonally across is Trinity Church (1877), Richardson's Romanesque Revival masterpiece, which was decorated by internationally known artists; and opposite the church stands the magnificent Boston Public Library (1895), designed in the Italian Renaissance style by Charles Follen McKim, of the preeminent New York firm of McKim, Mead & White. These three grand buildings, filled with the works of great artists, had been supported by Boston's wealthiest citizens, yet were open to, and enjoyed by, all.

Copley Square was also the starting point of Huntington Avenue, which projected diagonally west to Brookline, taking Bostonians deeper into reclaimed land and deeper into the cultural landscape. The first institution to build on Huntington was the Massachusetts Charitable Mechanic Association, which hired William Preston to design its mammoth brick Mechanics Hall in 1881. Symphony Hall was designed by McKim on a lot purchased by Major Higginson and friends in 1893. The venerable Massachusetts Horticultural Society made its new home opposite Symphony Hall in 1901, in a structure designed by the firm of Wheelwright and Haven.

Other musical institutions soon followed the Boston Symphony Orchestra to Huntington Avenue: the piano manufacturers Chickering Hall (1901), the New England Conservatory of Music (1902) and its Jordan Hall (1903), and the Boston Opera House (1909). (The Conservatory and the Opera House were financed by Eben Jordan, Jr., a philanthropist whose father had founded the Jordan Marsh Company.) By 1909, the Museum of Fine Arts had moved to Huntington as well, having long since outgrown its home in Copley Square.

The creation of what came to be called Boston's "Cultural Mile"—Huntington Avenue, from the old Museum of Fine Arts to the new—was not just a matter of fashion. It also made financial sense to build on this recently developed land. The land and construction for Horticultural Hall, for instance, cost $515,997; but the Horticultural Society had sold its old Tremont Street lot for $600,000, resulting in a tidy profit as well as a new space. At the opening of Symphony Hall, Major

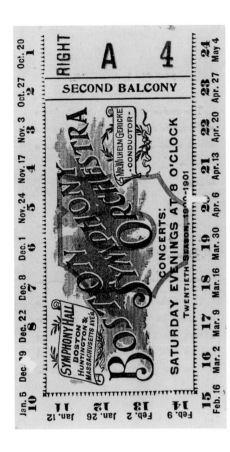

At left, this March 14, 1900, Boston Herald article describes the public and backstage spaces of Symphony Hall; above, a season ticket for Saturday evenings during the 1900-1901 season

BOSTON'S CULTURAL MILE

The movement of cultural and religious institutions into—then beyond—the Back Bay was in full swing by the 1870s, when the original Boston Museum of Fine Arts opened in Art (Copley) Square. Huntington Avenue, laid out in 1872, began at the square, and, as the century turned, a number of major Boston institutions moved to Huntington Avenue, many clustering around the intersection of Huntington and West Chester Park (renamed Massachusetts Avenue in 1894). So rich and grand were these architecturally impressive "palaces of the people" that Huntington Avenue, from the old Museum of Fine Arts (1876) to the new (1909), became known as Boston's Cultural Mile.

Symphony Hall (1900)

When the Boston Symphony Orchestra made its debut in 1881, its home was the old Boston Music Hall (1852) on Hamilton Place, whose current (and substantially altered) incarnation is the Orpheum Theater. When city planners threatened to lay a new street through the Music Hall in 1893, the Symphony's great benefactor, Henry Lee Higginson, negotiated the purchase of land on the corner of Huntington and West Chester Park. The architect Charles Follen McKim, of McKim, Mead & White, was aided by the acoustic expert Wallace Clement Sabine, an assistant professor of physics at Harvard. The original entrance, on Huntington, was moved around the corner some years after the Huntington Avenue underpass of the 1940s robbed the building of its original, more gracious, siting.

Isabella Stewart Gardner Museum (1903)

The art patron and avid collector, Isabella Stewart Gardner, and her husband, John Lowell Gardner, Jr., originally lived in Boston's Back Bay. Following her husband's death, Mrs. Gardner built Fenway Court at the corner of the Fenway and Worthington Road. Mrs. Gardner's "Venetian palace"—designed by its owner, with the assistance of Willard T. Sears—served as her home and private art museum, as well as a space for elite social gatherings and musical performances. The charming, independent, and strong-willed Mrs. Gardner frequently hired members of the Boston Symphony Orchestra to play for special events, including Fenway Court's much-heralded debut on January 1, 1903.

Boston Opera House (1909)

The Opera House was built by Eben Jordan, Jr.—the same philanthropist who helped finance Jordan Hall and the Emerson Majestic Theatre. Designed by Parkman B. Haven, of Wheelwright and Haven, this glorious building had 84 boxes and 2,750 seats. So tasteful and chaste was its exterior of red brick, gray limestone, and white terra cotta that one Boston music critic dubbed it "the first Unitarian Opera House." The building was demolished in 1958, to be replaced by Northeastern University dormitories.

Boston Museum of Fine Arts (1909)

In 1909, the Boston Museum of Fine Arts moved from its Copley Square location to its new home on the outer reaches of Huntington Avenue. Architect Guy Lowell was joined by R. Clipston Sturgis, Edmund M. Wheelwright, and D. Despradelle in designing this massive, granite, neoclassical building with Ionic temple portico and two flanking wings. Between 1911 and 1988, several structures were added, including the Evans Memorial Wing (1911-1915), the Decorative Arts Wing (1924-1928), and the West Wing (1981).

New England Conservatory of Music (1902)
Jordan Hall (1903)

The New England Conservatory of Music, the nation's first college of music, was founded in 1867. Though its classes were originally held in the old Music Hall on Hamilton Place— where the Boston Symphony Orchestra made its first home—the school moved, in 1882, to the elegant St. James Hotel, on Franklin Square in the South End. Two decades later, Wheelwright and Haven designed its present Classical Revival home on Huntington Avenue—deliberately and conveniently built

close to the new Symphony Hall. In 1881, Henry Lee Higginson asked nineteen members of its faculty to be section leaders in his new Boston Symphony Orchestra. To this day, a number of BSO musicians are on the faculty of the conservatory.

Jordan Hall, financed by, and named after, the NEC trustee Eben Jordan, Jr.—son of the founder of the Jordan Marsh department store—was added to the New England Conservatory of Music in 1903.

Christian Science Church (1906)

Fifteen years after Mary Baker Eddy founded the Church of Christ, Scientist, a small Romanesque Christian Science chapel (1894) was built near the corner of Massachusetts and Huntington avenues by the architect Franklin Welch. That modest beginning was augmented by a Classical Revival basilica—added in 1906 by the architects Charles E. Brigham and Solon S. Beman—then ultimately transformed into the current, block-long complex through the 1968–1973 work of I. M. Pei and Partners.

Horticultural Hall (1901)

The Massachusetts Horticultural Society was founded in 1829 to develop interest and expertise in the field of horticulture. Among its many achievements were the founding of Mount Auburn Cemetery in Cambridge (1831) and the mounting of an annual Flower Show, now world renowned. The society made its first headquarters on School Street (1844), followed by a Tremont Street building (1865) near the old Music Hall, off Boston Common. In January of 1900, it bought land opposite Symphony Hall and employed Boston's city architect, Edmund March Wheelwright—of the firm Wheelwright and Haven—to design this ornate English Baroque structure. Wheelwright's many local works include the nearby New England Conservatory and the Massachusetts Historical Society.

Chickering Hall (1901)

Opening shop in 1823, the entrepreneur Jonas Chickering made fine pianofortes that were sold and esteemed around the world. In 1852, fire destroyed his Washington Street factory; it was rebuilt on Tremont Street in the South End and once employed as many as 400 workers. On February 8, 1901, the firm opened Chickering Hall at 239 Huntington, next to Horticultural Hall, as a performance space. The building became the St. James Theatre (1912), then the Uptown movie theater. It was razed in 1968 to allow the expansion of the Christian Science Center. Chickering & Sons' business moved to New York in the 1930s.

Mechanics Hall (1881)

Shortly after Huntington Avenue was laid out, the Massachusetts Charitable Mechanic Association—founded in 1795, with Paul Revere as its first president—built Mechanics Hall on the corner of West Newton Street and Huntington. Designed by William Gibbons Preston, the mammoth red brick structure, decorated with medallions and terra cotta ornamentation, served as Boston's convention center for seventy-five years—and the home of "pop" concerts in the spring of 1900. Though Mechanics Hall was leveled in 1959 for the construction of the Prudential Center complex, Preston's work survives in buildings like the old Museum of Natural History, at Newbury and Berkeley streets, which now houses Louis clothing store.

Boston Public Library (1895)

The Boston Public Library was the nation's first major free public library. Originally on Mason Street (1854), then on the site of today's Colonial Theater (1858), the BPL moved into this noble Italian Renaissance–inspired building in 1895. Charles Follen McKim was commissioned to build this Copley Square "palace" on land donated by the state. The architect employed a dazzling army of artists to decorate his library, including Daniel Chester French, Puvis de Chavannes, John Singer Sargent, James McNeill Whistler, Edwin Austin Abbey, Louis and Augustus Saint-Gaudens, and Bela Pratt. The newer half of the library, with an entrance on Boylston Street, was designed by Philip Johnson in 1972.

Boston Museum of Fine Arts (1876)

Boston's first official art museum opened in Art Square (today's Copley Square) on America's centennial, July 4, 1876. Located where the Fairmont Copley Plaza Hotel now stands, and designed in red brick and terra cotta by John H. Sturgis and Charles Brigham, the MFA borrowed many of its earliest exhibits from the Boston Athenaeum. Despite additions to the building in 1879 and 1889, the museum was overflowing by 1899. In 1907, the trustees purchased twelve acres between Huntington Avenue and the Fenway and began to construct the museum's present home.

Higginson noted that his directors "chose this site as the best in Boston... and bought it at about half the price per foot paid for... Horticultural Hall."

THE WOMAN

Although women did not yet have the vote in 1900, they nevertheless were pursuing careers that had been almost unheard of a century before. Boston women had helped to create schools, from America's first kindergarten to Radcliffe College. They walked on union picket lines and were helping to educate, feed, and acculturate the needy in new institutions like Denison House, the North Bennet Street Industrial School, and the Women's Educational and Industrial Union. They were also writing symphonies and best-selling books, lecturing to large audiences, editing their own newspapers, running their own hospitals, and creating their own clubs—since they were not allowed past the threshold of the many men's clubs.

Isabella Stewart Gardner, a great supporter of the Boston Symphony Orchestra and patron of the arts

Of all these women, none captured the imagination—or garnered the headlines—as much as Isabella Stewart Gardner. Like Major Higginson, Isabella Stewart, although born in New York, was firmly linked to Boston by her life and work. Like Higginson, "Belle" had nourished her love for music in Vienna when young, then spent much of her adult fortune supporting the arts. She also maintained a close kinship to Harvard College. Most important, as the wife of the financier John Lowell Gardner, Jr., and as a close friend of Higginson, Mrs. Gardner supported the Major, the Symphony, and Symphony Hall through both the good times and bad.

Mrs. Gardner, popularly known as "Mrs. Jack," helped build and maintain Boston's musical credibility. She attended the seminal Harvard Musical Concerts at the old Music Hall on Hamilton Place and constructed lavish music rooms—first in her Back Bay home and later in Fenway Court—where she presented stellar musicians in classical concerts for her many friends. When Fenway Court opened in 1903, for example, she hired the Symphony's conductor, Wilhelm Gericke, and fifty of the orchestra's finest musicians to entertain her guests.

Mrs. Gardner praised Major Higginson's founding of the Symphony and publicly supported his decision to bring skilled musicians and conductors from abroad, despite protests from their American counterparts. She encouraged students at the New England Conservatory to become candidates for the orchestra and befriended talented musicians such as Gericke, Pops conductor Timothee Adamowski, and the established violinist Charles Loeffler. While many of her peers considered "popular" music vulgar, Mrs. Gardner enthusiastically backed the Major's decision to employ his musicians year-round by creating the Boston Pops, which offered "summer concerts of a lighter kind." From its first performance, in 1885, Pops was an immediate success. By 1901 the Pops—like the Symphony—were mainstays of the new Symphony Hall.

When proper Boston ladies were appalled by the scantily clad classical statues placed in the hall's gallery niches in 1903, Gardner was one of the few Symphony patrons who defended the use of nudity in art. And when World War I exacerbated anti-German sentiment in Boston, Mrs. Gardner and Major Higginson stood together in their unpopular and outspoken support of the German Karl Muck, the orchestra's conductor. (Muck conducted the Symphony from 1906 to 1908, then from 1912 to 1918. Though wrongly accused of spying for Germany, he was interned in an American camp before being allowed to return home.)

Mrs. Gardner was always happy to create a headline—especially if it helped the Major's musical endeavors. She outraged certain Boston Brahmins by attending a Pops concert wearing a hat-

MRS. "JACK'S" NEW RECORD.

She Pays $1120 for a $12 Symphony Concert Seat That She Wanted.

MRS. JOHN L. GARDNER,
Who has made a new record in the high premium paid for a Symphony Concert seat

Mrs. John L. Gardner is the reputed purchaser of the two $12 Symphony concert seats which sold at the record-breaking price of $1120 Thursday afternoon, and the incident is the talk of the day in Back Bay circles. The seats were bought by Mr. Connelly, the ticket agent, and at the time there was considerable speculation as to who the principal was.

The name of T. W. Lawson was at first connected with the transaction, but after it had been authentically learned that his seats were on the floor and had been bid in at a much more moderate price, it was pretty well understood that Mrs. "Jack" Gardner had established a new record for premiums.

This, it was thought, had some influence in the sale of the $7.50 seats for the Saturday evening Symphony concerts at yesterday's auction sale.

This sale opened promptly at 10 o'clock, and there was fully as large an attendance as at Thursday's $12 sale, a large number of ladies being present. Some of these made personal bids, but they usually started pretty low and were soon outclassed by their masculine competitors.

Initial bids of $1, $2 and $3, where they were entertained at all by the auctioneer, soon expanded to $7, $10 and even $15, and an unusually high average of premiums was received for every row sold.

One noticeable effect of the Gardner sale was that the second balcony seats located immediately above commanded a much higher premium than any other seats in that balcony, the premium in several cases amounting to $17.50.

The first seats to be offered yesterday morning were the nine rows at the rear of the $12 floor series. These brought a premium of from $4 to $12.50, the last four

seats sold commanding $4.50 each above the regular price.

Next came the five $7.50 rows at the rear of the first balcony. In Row E the premiums ranged from $7 to $12.50; in Row F from $7 to $9.50; in Row G from $5.75 to $8.75; in Row H from $4.75 to $7.50, and in Row I from $4.50 to $4.75.

The second balcony side seats were next auctioned off, beginning with Row A on the right looking toward the platform. These seats brought excellent prices, the first selling at $11 premium, and the price subsequently running up to $16, with a later drop to $10.

Row B on the same side also brought comparatively high bids, premiums ranging from $7 to $11, the central seats bringing $9 to $10.

When Row A on the opposite side was reached there was an immediate increase in interest. This is the row above the Gardner seats, and it brought high premiums right down to the very end.

The first two seats brought $12 each, the next four $13.50, and Nos. 7 to 13 all commanded $17.50 premium. After this there was a drop to $15.50 for Seats 14 and 15, and subsequently bids ranged from that figure down to $11.50.

The first bid in Row B started at $3, but the seat was knocked down at $12 premium, the same as the first one in Row A, and $2 more than the first seat in the corresponding row on the opposite side of the balcony.

From $12 the premiums for Row B seats sagged to $11 and finally $10.75, but it was still to be considered a bull market.

The remaining seats, those in the rear of the second balcony, also brought excellent prices. Altogether the concert sales have brought several thousands of dollars in premiums.

The newspaper account of the auction of season tickets at Symphony Hall in September, 1900; Isabella Stewart Gardner paid a previously unheard-of premium of $560 each for two $12 seats (first balcony right, A15 and A16).

HUB OF THE COMMUNITY

Although designed and built for the performance of orchestral music, Symphony Hall served as a social and civic center for many years. It was the premiere spot for a wide range of events: the Lodge-Lowell debate, mayoral inaugurations, Communist and Socialist party meetings, religious and travel lectures, and college commencements. The hall also held more social activities, such as book fairs and fashion and car shows.

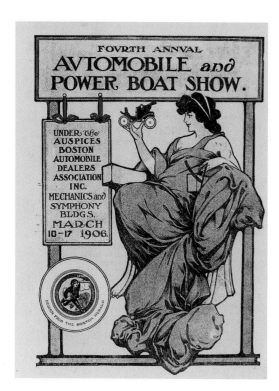

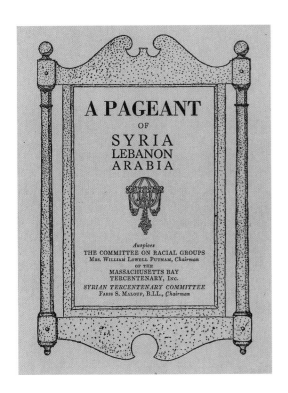

A PAGEANT
OF
SYRIA
LEBANON
ARABIA

Auspices
THE COMMITTEE ON RACIAL GROUPS
Mrs. William Lowell Putnam, *Chairman*
OF THE
MASSACHUSETTS BAY
TERCENTENARY, Inc.

SYRIAN TERCENTENARY COMMITTEE
Faris S. Malouf, B.LL., *Chairman*

OFFICIAL PROGRAMME
FOURTH SEMI-ANNUAL
Boston Shoe Style Show

Symphony Hall
BOSTON, MASS.
JULY 14 15 16 17

WILLIAM H. WALSH
DIRECTOR-MANAGER

NEW ENGLAND
ZIONIST REGION
presents

Dorothy Thompson
Wednesday Evening, April 29, 1942
SYMPHONY HALL
BOSTON, MASSACHUSETTS

If I forget thee, O Jerusalem, may
my right hand forget its cunning.
Psalm 137

Jordan Marsh

"Suddenly It's Spring"

A FASHION SHOW
IN FOUR SCENES

Presented by
Jordan Marsh Company
and Dedicated to
Women Who Work

THURSDAY EVENING
SEVEN TO NINE
Symphony Hall
MARCH 28, 1946

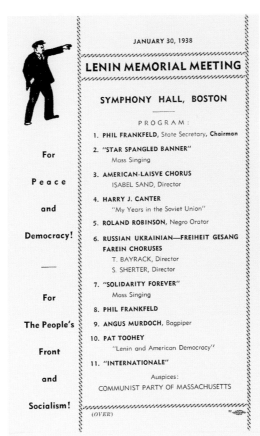

JANUARY 30, 1938

LENIN MEMORIAL MEETING

SYMPHONY HALL, BOSTON

PROGRAM:

For

Peace

and

Democracy!

———

For

The People's

Front

and

Socialism!

1. PHIL FRANKFELD, State Secretary, **Chairman**

2. "STAR SPANGLED BANNER"
   Mass Singing

3. AMERICAN-LAISVE CHORUS
   ISABEL SAND, Director

4. HARRY J. CANTER
   "My Years in the Soviet Union"

5. ROLAND ROBINSON, Negro Orator

6. RUSSIAN UKRAINIAN—FREIHEIT GESANG
   FAREIN CHORUSES
   T. BAYRACK, Director
   S. SHERTER, Director

7. "SOLIDARITY FOREVER"
   Mass Singing

8. PHIL FRANKFELD

9. ANGUS MURDOCH, Bagpiper

10. PAT TOOHEY
    "Lenin and American Democracy"

11. "INTERNATIONALE"
    Auspices:
    COMMUNIST PARTY OF MASSACHUSETTS

(OVER)

The Year of Peril
A SERIES OF WAR PAINTINGS BY Thomas Benton

SYMPHONY HALL
MASS. & HUNTINGTON AVE., BOSTON
BOSTON HERALD BOOK FAIR
OF NEW ENGLAND
OCT. 18-19-20-21
Doors Open 1:30 to 5 p.m. 7 to 11 p.m.
Speaking Sessions 3 p.m. 8:15 p.m.
EVENING, OCT. 19, 1943
Equiv. Price 35c 35¢
Tax Paid 3c

SPECULATORS OUTWITTED.

Applicants for 25=Cent Seats at the Symphony Concerts Must Present the Exact Change in Person at the Opening of the Doors.

THE NEW RULE OF ADMISSION TO THE SYMPHONY CONCERT.

MRS. ROTOLI'S HAT
LEADS TO
RUMPUS AT RECITAL.

Usher Insistent, Lady Indignant, Husband Talkative, Hat Not Removed.

Another hat incident happened yesterday afternoon in Symphony Hall, during Mme. Sembrich's recital. This time it was not Mrs. Apthorp who figured in it, but Signor Rotoli and Signora Rotoli.

Just after the beginning of the third part of the programme, an usher approached Signora Rotoli and requested that she remove her hat. He had previously stood in the aisle and made signals to the lady, of which she had declined to take notice. Then, crawling in over the knees of half a dozen ladies, he got within hailing distance and, with a very red face, asked that the hat be removed.

Signora Rotoli objected to removing her very becoming white plume, and, in distinct terms, told the usher so.

The request was repeated, ending with the usher's saying: "Remove yourself or remove your hat." Great indignation on the part of Signora Rotoli. Greater indignation on the part of Signor Rotoli. The usher retired. Signora Rotoli resumed at least an appearance of placidity. The portly signor, with true Italian vivacity, jumped to his feet and began addressing a young lady sitting two seats in the rear, who had evidently made the request for a wider range of vision. "No hat could be smaller," said the signor, eloquently. "You do not need it to be removed that you may see. You do not need it. You do not need it." Great interest among the ladies and many comments.

Usher Appears Again.

By this time Mme. Sembrich had begun singing again; but it looked as if she might have to stop.

Presently the usher approached again,

crawled over the six pairs of protruding knees, as before, and again spoke to the lady who wore the white hat. She removed her veil. "But do not take the hat off," said the signor; "you do not need to."

She did not.

The usher crawled back to his place by the door and summoned the head usher. Everybody felt uncomfortable, not knowing what would happen.

Signor Rotoli leaned over and patted his wife's white gloved hand, smiled at her reassuringly and held her hand in his for a few moments.

Sembrich finished and the Rotolis applauded heartily. Just before the last number they withdrew, and, walking straight to the office, the gallant signor complained of outrageously rude treatment received at the hands of the usher.

The head usher said, after the performance, that he should have felt obliged to enforce the ordinance to the end had not the incident happened so near the close of the programme.

The Recital.

Mme. Sembrich was assisted by Isidore Luckstone, accompanist. The programme was historical in character, beginning with Lotti, Paradies and other composers of the seventeenth century and extending to the present day, including some of the finest songs of Schubert, Schumann, Franz, Brahms and Tschaïkowsky.

The two Brahms songs perhaps made the most vivid impression; after these Mme. Sembrich obligingly gave, as an extra number, an unfamiliar song by Richard Strauss. There was also another extra number at the close of the recital. There was an immense audience.

Above, left, a newspaper story laments the problem with "speculators" who purchased discounted "rush" tickets and were caught selling them for full price in front of the hall. The policy was subsequently changed so that those buying "rush" tickets would have to enter the building immediately after purchasing them. Right, after a city ordinance, passed in 1898, prohibited men and women from wearing hats in "places of public amusement," there were many disagreements between patrons wearing hats and ushers trying to enforce the rule as described in this newspaper article from 1910.

band emblazoned "Oh you Red Sox," and personally boosted ticket sales—and prices—at Symphony Hall by submitting extravagant bids for her season tickets. A *Boston Post* headline marveled at the incident and impact of "MRS. 'JACK'S' NEW RECORD":

> *Mrs. John L. Gardner is the reputed purchaser of the two $12 Symphony concert seats which sold at the record-breaking price of $1120 Thursday afternoon, and the incident is the talk of the day in Back Bay circles. The seats were bought by Mr. Connelly, the ticket agent, and at the time there was considerable speculation as to who the principal was....*

> *Initial bids of $1, $2, and $3, where they were entertained at all by the auctioneer, soon expanded to $7, $10, and even $15.... One noticeable effect of the Gardner sale was that the second balcony seats located immediately above commanded a much higher premium.*

The Boston of 1900 was not the world it had once been. The Puritans were a misty memory. The literary Golden Age—of Emerson, Longfellow, and their friends—had already passed, as the nation's book center moved to Manhattan. Perhaps the most poignant indication that an era was truly ending was when the city's last horse-drawn streetcar made its final run on December 24, 1900.

But neither was Boston the modern city it would become. Innovations like automobiles, telephones, sound recordings, and moving pictures were in their infancy. Airplanes, radio programming, the World Series, and world wars were yet to come.

When Major Higginson addressed the audience at Symphony Hall on opening night in 1900, he was not yet sure what he and his colleagues had wrought:

The directors of this building have allowed me the honor and the pleasure of welcoming you to your new music hall.... The old Music Hall had become a great temple for our city, which had made many generations happy.... Whether this hall can ever give so much joy to our people as the old Music Hall no one can tell. Much depends on the public.

One hundred years later, we know the outcome well.

The public responded. The Major would be proud. ✍

—*Susan Wilson*

John Rockwell
I Was a Teenage Program-Passer

When I entered Harvard College in the fall of 1958, my serious interest in classical music was only a few years old. It had amounted to intense record collecting and pilgrimages to Salzburg and Aix-en-Provence, but also, in that first Cambridge autumn, a serious flirtation with the idea of majoring in music. I worked up my piano skills, such as they were, I was tutored in musicianship and ear-training with a young graduate student named Owen Jander (now a distinguished musicologist), and I took Elliott Forbes's Harmony 51, the prerequisite for all concentrators' music courses.

More recreationally, but still educationally, I started passing programs at Friday matinee concerts of the Boston Symphony in Symphony Hall. I forget how I made contact with the powers that be, but as I recall they had a program—or at least there was the opportunity—for students to usher or pass programs as part of a kind of BSO educational outreach program. Or maybe they just appreciated the cheap labor. What I know is that I appreciated the chance to hear a free concert every week and get paid a pittance as well. All I had to do was arrange my class schedule to avoid Friday afternoons and schlep into Boston and back on the creaking old subways.

Although I regretted not getting the chance to wear my own official purple uniform, as the ushers did, I opted for passing programs because that meant I could hear all the music. The ushers had to rotate, so that a group was on duty outside the main hall in case of a medical emergency, obstreperous latecomer, or whatever.

I got to stand, handing out my programs to the invariably polite, mostly aged, mostly female clientele until thirty seconds before the music was to begin. I would then dash upstairs and assume my position on the audience-right side of the balcony, as far forward as possible. I would have dashed for the left side (the pianists' hands, and all that), but I was stationed on the right side and would never have made it to the left in thirty seconds. Sometimes there would be a seat, into which I would gratefully slip. Otherwise, I stood. But I liked the right side, and while I missed the pianists' hands, I got to see their faces.

For me, almost directly above an orchestra and slightly upstage from the conductor has always been the ideal place to hear and see a concert. Hear, because the sound rises with an organic immediateness that I remember with pleasure (of course, it was the Boston Symphony and it was Symphony Hall). See, because a

part of the pleasure of regular attendance at an orchestra's concerts is to get to know the players, like the actors in an ensemble theater company—to see who's sitting a piece out or taking the solo, to observe the busywork of the intricate machine that an orchestra is.

Of course, there were pleasures, personal and sociological, in the actual passing of the programs. I can't remember the names of the veteran, professional ushers anymore, although I do recall the beefy, florid, friendly Irishman with whom I regularly stood in the line of duty. More vivid are some of the weekly Friday attendees. I'm sure the Brahmin ladies-who-lunch syndrome still prevails on Fridays, but forty-plus years ago it breathed of drawn curtains, ultra-proper manners, and Victorian fashions. Two ancient, frail, smiling sisters, dressed all in black, were a special pleasure to greet each week.

But the main pleasures were musical. The four years that I worked at Symphony Hall were Charles Munch's last four as music director of the orchestra. Compared with Arturo Toscanini, whose records I idolized and who had just retired and then died, Munch may not have been a great conductor. But he was an exciting, impassioned musician whose specialties extended far beyond Berlioz and Debussy and

Ravel to Mendelssohn, Brahms, and modern French composers.

The highlights were the grand Berlioz choral and quasi-operatic pieces; the Requiem, with the brass and massed timpani rattling the hall; and *La Damnation de Faust* and *Roméo et Juliette* and *L'Enfance du Christ*, along with the *Symphonie fantastique* and *Harold in Italy*. Usually, Munch used the Harvard-Radcliffe Choral Society, whose singing can still be heard on his recordings from that period. I remember a special pleasure, more romantic and vicariously lustful than musical or religious or college-patriotic, when Mephistofeles and Faust blasted through the huddling pack of Radcliffe nuns as they prayed and then squealed in terror during the final wild horseback ride of *La Damnation de Faust*.

Aside from records (and 25-cent seats in the San Francisco Municipal Auditorium a few years before, when Arthur Fiedler led summer Pops concerts in my hometown), I owe to the Boston Symphony my basic education in the depth and breadth of the orchestral repertory. When I look back on it now, the combination of a fine conductor, a great orchestra, and a great hall was a pretty good way to get that education. And passing the programs was fun, too.

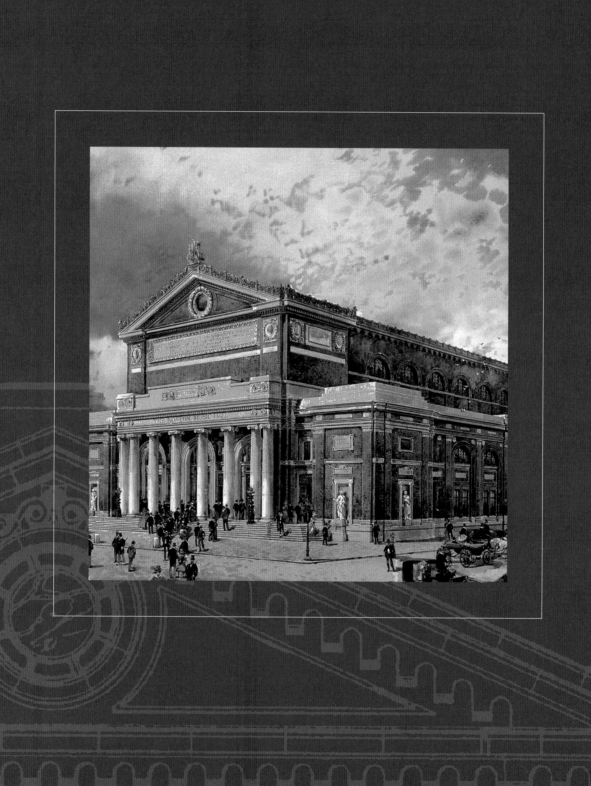

BRICKS AND MORTAR:
THE DESIGN OF
SYMPHONY HALL

One thinks of Symphony Hall, perhaps, as one thinks of those Boston ladies of the Victorian era who, it was said, hid their new gowns from Paris in the closet for a year so they wouldn't look too fashionable.

The frugal Henry Lee Higginson and his building committee stripped Symphony Hall of much of the stylish detail cherished by their New York architect, Charles Follen McKim. You can see the difference in the fine watercolor rendering of the building supplied by the architect's firm. Present in the rendering, but missing in the actual building, are many touches of luxury. It seems certain that McKim was disappointed, for he did not speak at the dedication. During construction, he wrote that his building had been "denuded by... ruthless economies."

It's true that Symphony Hall, viewed as an architectural object in the city, doesn't rank with McKim's masterpiece, the Boston Public Library. Yet in its quiet way, the Hall, too, is a masterpiece. Its understatement is part of what makes it so. One need only compare it to such confections as the Paris Opera or even the Boston Opera House, formerly the Savoy Theater on Washington Street, to realize that by the standards of the era, Symphony Hall was a simple, serious building. Its somewhat austere architecture tells you that it is a hall for music and not much else. It's not a place for gala parties or social climbing. It's about being inside listening, not about being outside looking. How appropriate, then, that its greatest claim to fame is its acoustics.

This is not to say that the Hall doesn't have its problems. There are times when you wonder whether an earlier generation didn't, perhaps, take a modest pleasure in the idea of suffering for art. The entrance and lobbies are cramped, the seats are narrow, backstage space is virtually nonexistent, and the exterior, to a generation raised on the lively graphics of TV, sometimes looks forbid-

The interior of Boston Music Hall after the
organ was removed and the sounding board
was installed, mid-1880s

ding. These are issues that need to be addressed as Symphony Hall moves into its second century. But the overall sense of a place unostentatiously dedicated to the experience of music will not, and need not, change.

Symphony Hall dates from Boston's architectural Golden Age. So much of what we cherish in the public realm of the city derives from a short burst of energy in a single generation, about the years 1875–1910. Symphony Hall, the Boston Public Library, Trinity Church, most of Commonwealth Avenue and the rest of the Back Bay, the Olmsted Emerald Necklace, the Museum of Fine Arts and the Gardner Museum, Holy Cross Cathedral and many other churches—even the great waterworks and pumping stations that in some years took half the municipal budget—all date from this period. It was an era of pride in the community and in the building of monuments to civic life—an era very different, in that regard, from today's more privatized society. Henry Lee Higginson was one of many wealthy Bostonians who, during this period, turned from making money to spending it for what was thought to be the public good.

Higginson, as is well known, founded the BSO and supported it financially for thirty-six years. The orchestra's first concert, on October 22, 1881, was held in the Music Hall in downtown Boston. The BSO played in the Music Hall for its first nineteen seasons. Nobody seems to have thought the building was a gem; it was called, in various contemporary comments, "a fire trap," "the breeziest and draftiest hall in the universe," "wretchedly ventilated," and "dangerous of egress." Higginson foresaw that someday he would have to build a new hall.

In 1892, with three friends, he purchased the property for the new music hall. At the time, the corner of Huntington and Massachusetts avenues (then called West Chester Park) must have seemed remote and forbidding. It was cut off from the Back Bay by the Boston and Albany Railroad

Charles Follen McKim (1847-1909)

and its yards (today's Amtrak line, now submerged beneath the Hynes Convention Center and the Prudential Center) and from the South End by the Providence and Boston railroad line (today's Orange Line). On the other hand, the land was relatively cheap at $170,000 for three-quarters of an acre. The choice of site, in fact, proved to be prescient. Symphony Hall, as events turned out, was the first of a chain of cultural institutions along Huntington Avenue, all of which opened between 1901 and 1909.

A crisis struck only a year after Higginson's acquisition of the site. The City of Boston announced that it intended to build an elevated railroad line directly through the Music Hall. As it happened, the proposal was eventually defeated at the polls. Nevertheless, it started the chain of events that led to the building of Symphony Hall several years later. Higginson acted quickly. In June 1893 he, with a group of other sponsors, issued a call for investors in a new corporation, to be capitalized at $400,000. The corporation would build and own a new hall. With the blissful, *Candide*-like innocence of many people who propose new buildings, Higginson announced, in July 1893, that the new hall would be ready in October 1894.

But who would be the architect? So far as is known, only one name was considered. Higginson had already been in touch, since October 1892, with Charles Follen McKim. Then forty-five, McKim was a founding partner in the architectural firm of McKim, Mead & White of New York. Before starting his own practice, McKim studied at Harvard (where, at first, he hoped to be a mining engineer) and at the École des Beaux-Arts in Paris. Both he and his future partner Stanford White worked for Henry Hobson Richardson, perhaps the greatest American architect of the second

The interior of the hall soon after its opening. Not all of the statues are in their niches, and the clerestory windows are in their original, uncovered, state.

Interior and exterior views of the Leipzig Gewandhaus (1884-1944); it was destroyed by bombing during World War II.

half of the nineteenth century, and both participated in the design of Richardson's Trinity Church on Copley Square. Acting with his usual foresight, Higginson made what was probably the best choice of an architect he could possibly have made at the time, and he did so even though much of McKim's best work still lay in the future. No doubt Higginson had checked out his choice with his colleagues. But there was no elaborate selection process like the one held a few years earlier for the Neues Gewandhaus in Leipzig, Germany, when seventy-five architects submitted designs in a competition. McKim was the Old Boy network's choice.

McKim doesn't quite rank with his mentor Richardson, but he belongs on any list of the two dozen or so great American architects. By the 1890s, McKim, Mead & White was the leading, trend-setting firm in America, the practitioners of a style usually known today as American Renaissance. This was an architecture that drew on the work of the Italian Renaissance to satisfy an American public that was becoming more sophisticated and more widely traveled—the same new public that was supporting European music at the Symphony and European painting and sculpture at the Museum of Fine Arts. Although inspired by the Renaissance, McKim's buildings frequently suggest the Georgian and Federal architecture of early America, in part because they are often executed in red brick, a material not common in Italy.

So fond of Europe was McKim that he founded the American Academy in Rome for the purpose, originally, of making sure that talented young architects would be immersed in the study of what he regarded as the great examples of architecture. McKim's masterpiece, as already noted, is the Boston Public Library of 1895, modeled on Italian Renaissance palazzos and also, as a sort of second-generation source, on the Bibliothèque Geneviève in Paris, which itself is a neo-Renaissance design by a Beaux-Arts architect of the nineteenth century. McKim built much for Harvard, including Robinson Hall, the Union, the Harvard Club of New York, and the Harvard Stadium. As early as 1890, he designed the Johnston Gate, at the west edge of Harvard Yard, for which he invented what came to be known (and still is known) as Harvard Brick: brick that is struck and burned in such a way that it resembles the antique brick used in the college's early buildings. In New York, McKim, Mead & White created such landmarks as Pennsylvania Station and the Villard Houses. White was notoriously murdered in 1906, and McKim retired in 1908, but the firm survived and, as late as the 1920s, designed the Harvard Business School.

Higginson's first letter to McKim is amusingly tentative. He was careful not to get in too deep, too soon. Like a skilled fly-caster, he merely flicked the bait across the water. "No hall is intended yet, and perhaps never," he wrote, but "perhaps you may have time to glance at the land." He called the site "the only feasible lot in Boston for a Music Hall."

McKim, of course, leaped at the lure, replying instantly and laying on the salesmanship quite thick: "We all feel that it is quite impossible to express the pleasure that we have that you should wish to associate us with the development of your splendid idea for a Music Hall... nothing more flattering or complimentary has ever happened to our office." Two weeks later he added, "There isn't a day I don't dream about the Music Hall."

This early correspondence demonstrates that Higginson already knew exactly what kind of hall he wanted. Architects always say they do their best work only with the help of a strong client. Higginson qualified. From day one, he produced what the author Richard Poate Stebbins calls "a detailed syllabus of the features appropriate for a music hall to house the Boston Symphony Orchestra." He listed criteria: The hall should provide seating for 2,200 to 2,500 people (fewer than the old Music Hall's 2,600); there should be a stage for ninety musicians; space must be left for an organ on the rear wall; and the hall should be lighted only "from windows in the top or in the highest part of the side walls." He even delved into architectural details, such as "a sounding board of some kind or a stage shut in by an alcove, rounded or angular." He expressed his preference for "round-arched Norman or Lombard architecture" and for "brick and brick ornament." "I always like the severe in architecture, music, men and women, books, etc.," he told his architect. Eight years later, Symphony Hall opened with every one of these features and preferences pretty much in place (although the seating rose to 2,625), including the somewhat too small stage (today's orchestra usually numbers well over one hundred).

Despite Higginson's warning that "I've no present purpose of building," McKim set to work. While visiting Paris, he hired the services of a young American who had been studying at the École des Beaux-Arts and who had also been helping in negotiations with the artist Puvis de Chavannes over murals for the Boston Public Library. The young architect was the talented John Galen Howard, who, a decade later, was to design the campus plan and early buildings of the University of California at Berkeley. Howard, it is believed, drew up for McKim three different generic concepts for a music hall. One was a semicircle, the shape of a classical Greek amphitheater. One was an ellipse, which a Beaux-Arts professor of Howard's thought would offer the best acoustics (an opinion that would horrify modern acousticians). One was a rectangle, like the Gewandhaus in Leipzig and the old Boston Music Hall. McKim's favorite was the amphitheater. Based on these studies, McKim's partner William R. Mead wrote Higginson that a hall could be built for a bare minimum of $300,000.

At that moment came the alarming proposal for the elevated railway, threatening to demolish the Music Hall. Higginson responded, as noted, by creating a corporation to build a new hall for $400,000, a figure that may have included reimbursement for the cost of the site. The appeal was successful: $402,000 was subscribed in only ten days (roughly $7.5 million in today's dollars). This remarkable outpouring occurred during the onset of the Panic of '93, one of the worst recessions in American history.

After this fast start, however, events slowed, partly because the railway proposal was killed in an autumn referendum and partly because the economy was going south. Higginson declared an indefinite moratorium. McKim nevertheless requested and received $1,200 to build an elaborate wood and plaster model of the future hall. In January 1894 it went on public exhibition in the unfinished Boston Public Library. It was a model of the interior only, enclosed in a box twelve feet square and seven feet high, so positioned that visitors could poke their heads up through a trap door in the floor to view the proposed auditorium. The form of that space was McKim's Greek theater, with curving tiers of seats for the audience and, behind a proscenium arch, more tiers for the players. Niches for classical statues ringed the upper wall.

It soon became obvious that the hall's sponsors weren't sold on the Greek theater concept. McKim had promised that "the wedge-form walls and the succession of rising arches immediately behind and above the orchestra offer a series of sounding boards of the best." But the halls the sponsors knew and trusted, such as the Grosser Musikvereinsaal in Vienna and the Neues Gewandhaus in Leipzig, were rectangles. Higginson said that the amphitheater "included some innovations, and

McKim's initial, conceptual models of the Greek theater plan, displayed at the Boston Public Library: left, the view toward the stage; and right, the view facing the rear of the hall

the directors were afraid to adopt it." McKim continued to push for his scheme: "Until I know positively from you that the form of the Greek theater must go, I propose to cherish my faith in it."

Four years of the moratorium passed before, in an improved economy, a purchaser finally appeared for the old Music Hall. In 1898, the plans for a new hall were revived. Higginson hadn't changed his mind in the interim. He wrote McKim: "While we hanker for the Greek theatre plan, we think the risk too great as regards results." He asked his conductor, Wilhelm Gericke, to procure plans and dimensions of the halls in Vienna and Leipzig. He asked McKim whether he wished to

New Boston Music Hall stock certificate,
issued on December 21, 1893

remain as the architect for a hall that, warned Higginson, must be "devoid of poetry and charm" and must be built for $200,000. McKim agreed to stay on the job. From this point on, the Leipzig Gewandhaus became the chief model. McKim went so far as to suggest taking the Gewandhaus dimensions—height, length, and width—and simply multiplying them by 1.3 to achieve a greater number of seats. Fortunately, such a hall was not built. So great a volume would have been too reverberant.

At this juncture, McKim was joined by a new figure, Wallace Sabine. Socrates said that the wise man is one who associates with those wiser than himself. McKim apparently recognized in Sabine someone who knew more about acoustics than he would ever know, and accepted him as virtual co-architect. Sabine was a young professor of physics at Harvard who more or less invented the science of acoustics as a result of trying to improve the sound in the auditorium of Harvard's old Fogg Museum (later this building became part of the school of architecture and was renamed Hunt Hall, after its architect). Now demolished, the Fogg auditorium still lives in many persons' memories, including that of this writer, as an almost uniquely terrible space for acoustics. While investigating the acoustics of the Fogg and other Harvard rooms, Sabine developed the first formula for predicting reverberation time. President Eliot of Harvard, impressed, recommended him to Higginson as acoustical consultant.

The Fogg Auditorium was a Greek theater in form, with curved seating and a curving back wall. It has often been assumed that Sabine's experience with the Fogg led him to kill McKim's amphitheater. Research by Stebbins, however, makes it clear that the amphitheater proposal was abandoned before Sabine became involved. Sabine soon made many critical suggestions to McKim, one of which was to squelch the idea of simply inflating the Leipzig Gewandhaus. He also urged that

Leo Beranek

The Acoustics of Symphony Hall

Wallace C. Sabine (1863-1919)

Dr. Leo Beranek, a noted acoustician, maintains that there are six acoustical parameters that must be satisfied in the audience areas in a concert hall: reverberation time, acoustical intimacy, acoustical spaciousness, diffuseness of the reverberant sound field, loudness, and bass response. According to Beranek, all of these factors were addressed in the construction of Symphony Hall, thereby ensuring the highly-regarded acoustics. He explains the technical aspects of the acoustical parameters in this essay:

The optimum reverberation time in a concert hall for today's symphonic repertoire lies between 1.8 and 2.0 seconds—in Symphony Hall it is 1.9 seconds. Once the reverberation time was decided to equal that of the old Music Hall, Wallace Sabine used his formula to determine the cubic volume of the hall, given the area of the audience and the building material for the wall and the ceiling.

Acoustical intimacy and acoustical spaciousness are dependent on the architectural style of the hall. The models chosen by the Building Committee, namely the Leipzig Gewandhaus and the old Boston Music Hall were optimal. Those halls and Symphony Hall are a "shoe-box" shape and are narrow and not too long. Symphony Hall is 75 feet in width, and the distance from the front of the stage to the farthest listener is 138 feet, about the maximum for good sight. A wide hall will lack acoustical intimacy. A hall with a fan-shaped audience space will lack "acoustical spaciousness" because music from the stage that reaches the sidewalls will be reflected toward the back corners of the audience rather than toward the main seating areas. In the Tanglewood Music Shed, which is fan shaped; this problem is overcome by the inclusion and particular design of the suspended acoustical panels over the orchestra and the audience areas.

The diffuseness of the reverberant sound field is created by architectural irregularities, that is to say, by niches and irregularities on the sidewalls, coffers in the ceiling, and irregular balcony fronts, or their modern architectural equivalents. These architectural features are present in Symphony Hall.

Sufficient loudness depends on both a proper reverberation time and an audience size that is not too large. One must reason that if an audience is large, the portion of the sound from the orchestra that reaches each person will be less than if the audience is small. The late Herbert von Karajan, frequent conductor of the Vienna Philharmonic Orchestra, said he preferred Boston's hall to Vienna's because the sound of Romantic music was too loud in Vienna.

The bass response depends on the materials of the walls and ceiling, as well as the thickness of the upholstering of the seats. In Symphony Hall the walls are plaster above the second balcony, and plaster on concrete below. Only the stage enclosure is wooden. This wood will absorb bass sound. If wood is used in a hall, other than in small amounts, it must be thick and cemented to a solid concrete backing. The upholstering of seats should be the minimum necessary for comfort. Thick upholstering absorbs bass tones. The uncomfortable, thinly upholstered seats of Symphony Hall are thus an acoustical advantage.

In addition to those six parameters, the orchestra must be placed in a stage house, or beneath a canopy, or in some type of building structure that melds the music from the vari-

ABSORBING POWER.

	Leipzig Gewandhaus.	Boston Music Hall, Old.	Boston Music Hall, New.
Plaster on lath.	73	100	34
Plaster on tile.	0	0	46
Glass.	0.4	1.5	0.6
Wood.	14	47	38
Drapery.	18	0.6	0
Audience.	667	1,052	1,135
Orchestra.	38	38	38
Total = a.	810	1,239	1,292

V and a being determined for each of the three halls, the duration, T, of the residual sound after standard initial intensity can be calculated.

The results, in seconds, are as follows :—

Leipzig Gewandhaus.............................. 2.30
Old Boston Music Hall........................... 2.44
New Boston Music Hall........................... 2.31

In other words, the new hall, although having a seating-capacity for over a thousand more than the Gewandhaus and nearly two hundred more than the old hall, will have a reverberation between the two. and nearer that of the Gewandhaus than that of the old hall.

It is interesting to contrast this with the result that would have been obtained had the plan been followed of reproducing on an enlarged scale the Gewandhaus. Assuming perfect reproduction of all proportions with like materials, the volume would have been 25,300 cubic metres, and the absorbing power 1,370. resulting in the value, $T = 3.02$. This would have differed from the chosen result by an amount that would have been very noticeable.

The new Boston Music Hall is, therefore, not a copy of the Gewandhaus, but the desired results have been attained in a very different way.

ous sections equally and that enables the musicians to hear each other. Also, the orchestral music must be distributed equally to all parts of the hall, and then there must be no echoes.

Finally, noise is controlled by proper design of the heating, air-conditioning and ventilating system, and by proper building construction to eliminate noise and vibration from traffic and aircraft outside.

In summary, four crucial decisions were responsible for the success of Symphony Hall. First, excellent concert halls were chosen as models, and their properties were incorporated into Symphony Hall. Second, the proper reverberation time was achieved through the use of Sabine's reverberation formula. Third, the length of the hall as first presented by McKim was shortened by Sabine's recommendation that the four sets of boxes be eliminated and a second balcony be substituted and by Higginson's decision to reduce the spaces between the rows of seats by five inches. And, finally, Sabine designed an excellent stage house for the orchestra.

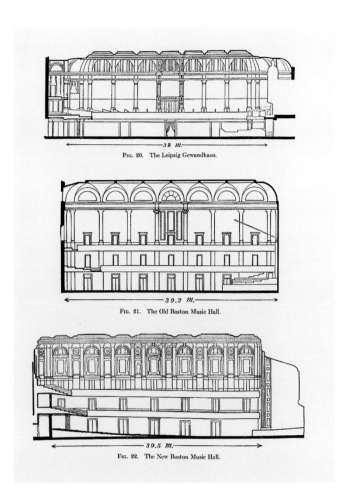

FIG. 20. The Leipzig Gewandhaus.

FIG. 21. The Old Boston Music Hall.

FIG. 22. The New Boston Music Hall.

At left, a comparison of sound absorbtion characteristics among the Leipzig Gewandhaus, the "old" Boston Music Hall, and the "new" Boston Music Hall, from Sabine's papers

At left, a comparison of sound absorption from Sabine's papers on acoustics

surfaces be broken up and angled. Thus, for example, the niches for statuary, carried over from the Greek design, were important acoustically. The hall's coffered ceiling, so remarkably varied in its shapes, is another instance of this principle. Sabine announced that curves were bad for sound (because they tend to focus it) and that the stage area should be enclosed under a ceiling lower than that of the rest of the hall.

The hall now went through a series of permutations, getting longer and shorter as its designers tried to balance the number of seats against the quality of the sound and the sightlines. All the designs were based on the proportions of Leipzig, but with constant reference also to the old Music Hall. Higginson later wrote that "the real discussion was based on only two buildings—the present Boston Music Hall and the Leipzig Gewandhaus." Sabine invented a quiet heating and ventilating system, in which air would drop silently from the ceiling to be drawn out through the floor. Most important, perhaps, he helped shape the stage enclosure. He wrote that the orchestra was placed "in a somewhat contracted stage recess, from the side walls of which the reflection is better because they are nearer [to the players] and not occupied by an audience." Sloping walls, floor, and (in part) ceiling project the music forward to the audience. Sabine warned that the sound would suffer if the stage were enlarged so that performers were placed in front of the proscenium—although when choruses are used, this displacement often does occur—even at Symphony Hall's inaugural concert.

In March 1899 the final drawings were delivered, including the well-known watercolor view seen from the southeast corner of Massachusetts and Huntington avenues. A center aisle was added for the front section of orchestra seats. Higginson asked that a chamber music hall, for 600 to 700, be stuffed into the building at the rear of the second balcony. McKim suggested a location

McKIM, MEAD & WHITE

SCALE 0 5 10 15 20 25 30 FEET

FRONT ELEVATION

Charles Follen McKim: This front elevation and section through the hall shows the "box" nesting within the larger "box."

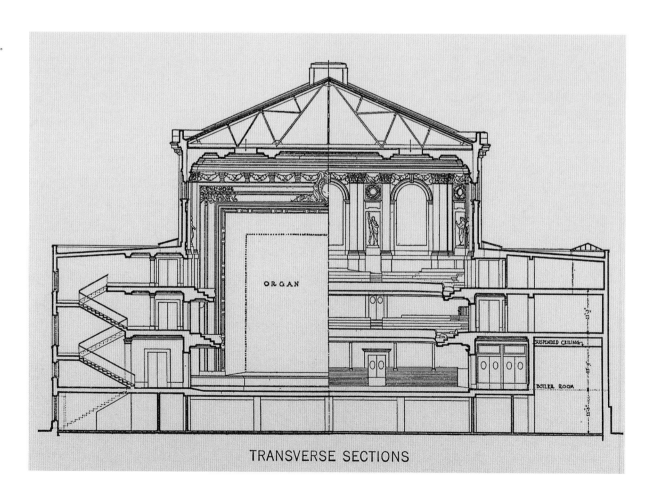

ORGAN

SUSPENDED CEILING

BOILER ROOM

TRANSVERSE SECTIONS

Sam Allis

The Sitting Experience

Enough about the acoustics. We *know* they are nonpareil. What about the business end of the listening experience—the seats? Along with our ears, our derrières inform our judgments of an evening here, too. And there are, quite simply, no seats quite like the ones at Symphony Hall. They are invaluable artifacts of urban archaeology because they tell us much about the Brahmins who built the place and then flocked to it like gulls. What we can glean is that these people demanded capacious legroom but otherwise luxuriated in discomfort—an affliction that can be traced to Cotton Mather. Surely, no other seats in the world afford such a schizoid listening experience.

First, the legroom: By airline standards, the symphony seat hovers somewhere between Business and First Class. Absolutely boffo after the Delta Shuttle. The neophyte instinctively brings his knees to a ninety-degree angle when he first sits down, assuming he is trapped in a fugue state of Economy Class hell at 30,000 feet. But then a strange thing happens. He relaxes and gingerly slides his feet toward the seat ahead. No one barks at him. There is still daylight between his knees and the back of the aforementioned seat. He probes further until, *mirabile dictu,* his legs are fully outstretched. Can this be, he wonders? Can I actually sit through a concert without contracting cramps?

Yes, thanks to Major Higginson and his troops. Proper Bostonians of both sexes were spawned long and lanky back then. Their limbs, in general, and legs, in particular, were endless. They needed extra real estate for them—expected extra real estate for them—and were happy to pay for it. God bless them.

Sadly, the same encomium does not apply to the seats themselves—humorless things of black leather stuffed with modest tufts of horsehair and rimmed with brass tacks. They are noteworthy for their near complete absence of padding. This shortage leads to a sporadic shifting of weight in the first movement of a concerto that routinely becomes pandemic by the fourth.

The situation is particularly trying during programs without intermissions. A performance of Mahler's Second Symphony, for example, lasts longer than a Celtics game. While the musical confection is entrancing, the physical challenge is stiff.

Not everyone succumbs to the seats without a fight. A few savvy souls sport pillows of wondrous shapes

The leather seats of Symphony Hall are important to the acoustics.

and sizes when they attend concerts. While such behavior may appear odd to the unenlightened, Symphony veterans know there is much to be said for such stratagems. And as more aging baby boomers find their lower backs reduced to aspic from years of maniacal exercise, we should expect to see a profusion of pillows in the future. In the meantime, one could do worse than to sit on one's coat.

There has been much speculation about why the seats at Symphony Hall are so uncomfortable. One obvious theory is that they keep everyone awake. While a generous number of audience members may

rest their eyes at one point or another during a concert, it is damned hard to take an extended nap. Then, too, there is the cultural explanation: The Brahmins have always abhorred luxury. They were hardwired at Plymouth Rock to endure discomfort in the name of moral rectitude, and they have done one hell of a job in that regard thus far. To sit on plush, cushioned affairs would be wrong, wrong, wrong.

Whatever the case, the seats are here to keep us honest. And if they are a pain in the derrière, isn't that a small price to pay for world-class musical fare?

"BMH" cast in the balustrade; the hall was originally to be called Boston Music Hall.

off the first balcony instead, and, although the idea was abandoned, it partly survives as today's Cabot-Cahners Room.

As with most buildings, costs kept rising. To keep within sight of the budget, cuts were made. Gone are McKim's exterior statuary, slate roof, harp-shaped finial that would have crowned the roof, carved inscriptions, and decorative eaves like those at the Boston Public Library. It's interesting to note, in this connection, Higginson's comment about McKim in a letter to Harvard's president Charles Eliot: "If… looked after, [McKim] will restrain his desire for ornament." A key element of the architect's proposed decor was a large limestone panel over the Huntington Avenue entrance, which was to bear the carved words "Boston Music Hall." But now that the old Music Hall was to be renovated by a new owner, the new building would need another name. "Higginson Hall" was one suggestion. Whatever Higginson thought of this idea, the fact is that the panel has remained

PLANS FOR MODERN MUSIC HALL.

Architects Submit Drawings Embodying Suggestions for an Auditorium With Fine Acoustic Properties.

ARCHITECT'S PLAN OF A MUSIC HALL.

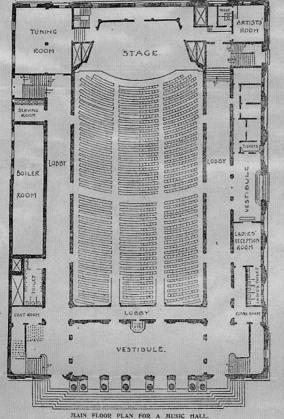

MAIN FLOOR PLAN FOR A MUSIC HALL.

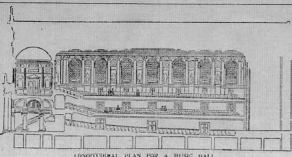

LONGITUDINAL PLAN FOR A MUSIC HALL.

The March 14, 1899 Boston Globe description of the stockholder presentation of the design of the new hall by Higginson and the architects. It was the first time the public could see the layout of the building (the floor plan shows no center aisle in the front orchestra section, as was added by Higginson shortly before the hall was built).

At right, above, decorative grillwork of the first balcony; below, two views of the coffered ceiling. The detailing of both balcony and ceiling are important factors in the hall's acoustics.

rather dispiritingly blank until recently—plans are now underway to engrave the panel. (Before it was realized that the building's name must change, the letters BMH, for Boston Music Hall, were cast in the iron stair railings, where they can be seen today.) The name "Symphony Hall" seems never to have been formally designated. It simply caught on.

Budget constraints were severe. Not all of the money originally pledged was redeemed, and a mortgage of $325,000 was eventually required. The final cost of the hall, budgeted at $200,000, was $583,000 exclusive of land—$11 million in today's dollars (it was nevertheless a fifth the cost of the Boston Public Library). It was constructed by Norcross Brothers of Worcester, one of the best builders in U.S. history; the firm also built much of the architecture of H. H. Richardson. There were the usual unpredicted problems. Spruce piles, originally specified, broke off when driven into the hard gravel subsoil; concrete footings were substituted. There was a brief panic over a steel shortage. Nevertheless, construction was both excellent and rapid. Ground was broken on June 9, 1899, and the hall was opened to the public on September 20, 1900—a period of less than sixteen months.

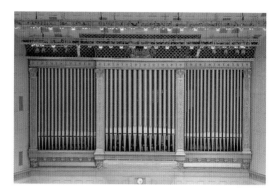

The original ornamental pipes of the Symphony Hall organ were part of the decorative design of the hall; a new Aeolian Skinner organ replaced the George Hutchings original in 1949. Below, a newspaper describes Symphony Hall's organ as the finest in the world.

The original organ (which has since been replaced) was designed and built by a prominent firm. The ever-helpful Sabine, however, revised the design, announcing that the instrument would sound better. "I was making organs before he was born!" was the response of the designer, who nevertheless later admitted that Sabine had been right. Sabine, though, miscalculated the hall's reverberation. He predicted a reverberation time of 2.3 seconds at mid-frequency with a full audience. The actual figure is about 1.85. But since Sabine made the same error in calculating the reverberation of the other halls he studied, the error didn't matter. Symphony Hall sounded, as intended, much like the great European halls. It was, however, criticized by some for not being loud enough. The acoustical expert Dr. Leo Beranek suggests the reason was that Symphony Hall was much larger than the European halls, which average 1,400 seats, yet had the same size orchestra. As the orchestra grew larger over the years, the criticism disappeared.

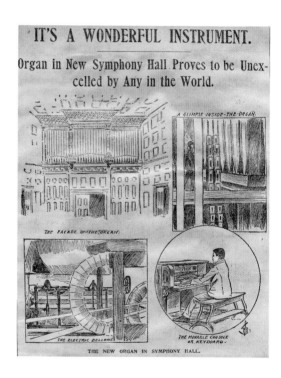

Symphony Hall opened for public inspection three weeks before the inaugural concert. At the time, only one of the statues in the niches was present. Although the original color scheme was cream and gold, a recent sampling revealed that parts of the hall interior have been painted countless times and in a variety of colors. It appears that in the early years, the lower walls may have been painted red in the winter, then changed to green for the Pops season. Newspapers at the opening generally praised the tasteful simplicity of the interior. There have, however, always been nay-sayers. A New York paper in 1900 said of the auditorium: "It must be visited to learn of its cheerlessness," and, ninety years later, the New York critic Paul Goldberger wrote that the exterior looked like "a vast warehouse or train station."

The inaugural concert, of course, was held on October 15, 1900. Gericke conducted the orchestra and a chorus of 250 in a program that featured Beethoven's *Missa Solemnis*. There was a speech by Higginson and a terrible poem by Owen Wister, soon to write the novel *The Virginian* and later a president of Boston's Tavern Club. It began:

> Yea, sweep thy harp which hath a thousand strings!
> The joy that sometimes is in darkest night,
> And the strange sadness which the sunshine brings,
> The splendors and the shadows of our inward sight,—
> All thee within thy weaving harmonies unite.

NEW SYMPHONY HALL A PLACE OF BEAUTY.

Perfect in All Requirements, a Delight to the Eye and Heart—New Scheme in Ventilation and Heating—Acoustic Properties Perfect.

Cast decorative banister and newel post

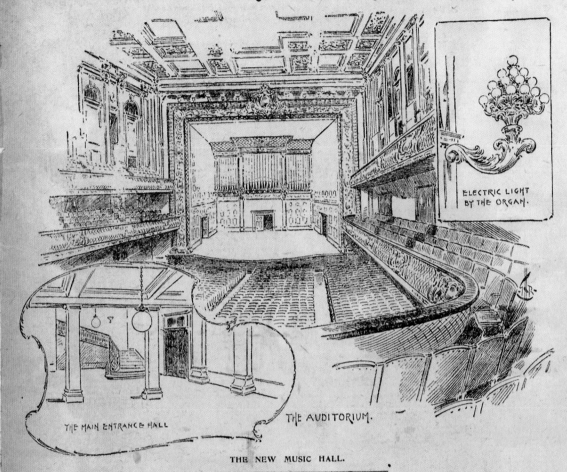

ELECTRIC LIGHT BY THE ORGAN.

THE MAIN ENTRANCE HALL

THE AUDITORIUM.

THE NEW MUSIC HALL.

The new Symphony hall is a thing of beauty, and doubtless is will be a joy for many a year to come, if not forever.

It is located at the corner of Huntington and Massachusetts avs. Its doors were thrown open last evening to allow of its inspection by local newspaper men, and the general verdict seemed to be that the hall is perfect in all conceivable requirements.

It is not a place of glittering splendor to dazzle the eyes of a visitor for a time and to send him home with a headache from the contemplation of a medley of gaudy coloring and "myriads of lights" as the enthusiastic observer often terms them; but it is a stately, beautifully proportioned hall, the atmosphere of which warms one's heart the moment the threshold is crossed, and will inevitably leave a pang of regret when the hour to leave it has arrived.

The first impression received upon entering the new hall is one of surprise that architecturally it differs so slightly from old Music hall. The resemblance, in its various proportions, is so marked that one might easily imagine it the old hall in a brand new, up-to-date dress.

The fact is the new hall is but one foot narrower and 10 feet longer than the old, while the ceiling is only six feet lower.

The two balconies have much the same effect to the casual glance as those in the old hall, although they are really both considerably lower, and they slope downward toward the stage—which those in the old hall did not—greatly improving the facilities for seeing and hearing.

The floor of the auditorium, unlike that of the old hall, has a gradual incline like that of the average theater, so that everyone can have a view of the stage.

The stage is considerably lower than the stage of the old hall and utterly at variance with it in every other way. It resembles what is called a box scene, on the dramatic stage, that is, completely closed up in the rear at the top and on both sides; but in this case the "boxing" instead of being merely "canvas" painted to represent the interior walls of an apartment, is panelled wood.

The organ occupies the entire space at the back of the stage, which is about feet wide.

he most beautiful feature of the hall he proscenium arch, which though gestive of the customary theater ch, is much handsomer, richer and

more artistic than any theater arch that Boston has ever had.

This arch is actually a magnified gold picture frame, of the same general shape that one would see on a very expensive oil painting, the portion of the molding in relief representing garlands of laurel leaf and of interwoven fruits, while the receding surface bears a notably beautiful renaissance arabesque, comprised mainly of acanthus vines and blossoms.

Directly in the center of the top of the arch is a graceful antique shield, bearing the name "Beethoven," and on either side of it a conventionalized cornucopia containing the customary symbols of plenty.

Rare Decorative Scheme.

There are three exits from the stage, for the artists, one on either side and one directly through the middle of the organ, all communicating with a wide corridor, which in turn leads to various spacious and airy dressing rooms and to the tuning room of the musicians at the left of the stage, where there are upward of 100 lockers.

Thanks to electricity, the organist, who has been deprived of his customary seat by the middle door just referred to, is able to trundle his seat of operations around with him to any part of the house—even to the rear of the second balcony, should he take the notion, a flexible cable of electric wires being all the communication he requires with his organ to make it discourse most eloquently.

The decorative scheme throughout the hall is a continual and ever-increasing delight to the eye, the prevailing tone being pale gray, slightly graded here and there.

The chairs, which are particularly comfortable, are upholstered in dark olive green leather, and the only touches of brilliancy in the whole house are furnished by the rich mahogany doors, studded with brass nails; the walls of the first floor, which are of a dead though warm red; the upholstering of balcony railings, also red, and the fronts of the balconies and the proscenium arch, which are of gold.

The balcony fronts are not flat, but gracefully rounded; are dotted with odd shaped shields, for the names of the great masters in music, and supported by cupids which are not quite in the "altogether."

Although the hall is brilliantly illuminated, with the exception of two beautiful bronze electric brackets on the front of the organ, the lights are arranged so as to be within the range of vision of the auditors.

The musicians bask in the effulgence shed by a row of concealed side lights behind the molding of the proscenium frame, while the auditorium is lighted by five clusters close up to the ceiling.

The acoustic properties of the hall, which are solely the result of the plans of Prof Wallace C. Sabine of Harvard university, appear to be absolutely faultless.

Two individuals, last evening, one standing at the rear of the hall in the upper gallery, the other on the stage, conversed in a low conversational tone without the slightest raising of the voice, and each heard the other distinctly.

It is worthy of note that Prof Sabine remarked before the plans were drawn for the hall, that he would guarantee to furnish just what he has produced, and that he declined to admit the possibility of failure.

The organ, which was tried last night, the first selection being Mendelssohn's wedding march, proved to be a remarkably sweet and melodious as well as powerful instrument. Its human voice tones are startling in their natural quality.

The organ will be used in the symphony concerts, something that has not hitherto been done in Boston.

The most curious thing about the new hall is the system of ventilation and heating, for which great things are promised. Contrary to all old-fashioned theories and notions the heat is brought down from the ceiling and the bad air is drawn off close to the floor, and the way it is accomplished is interesting.

In the top of the building, directly above the stage, is an apartment 60 feet long and 20 wide, the windows of which are to be entirely open the year around allowing the free ingress of air uncontaminated by the city streets.

From this apartment a well extends down to a network of steam pipes in the cellar. Behind these pipes are two immense fans which draw a perfect whirlwind of cold air down the well from the roof across the surface of the steam pipes, where it becomes moderately heated, and then carry it up another well to a big reservoir above the ceiling of the auditorium.

No Drafts.

Meanwhile, another set of fans in the basement is drawing out the air of the lower part of the auditorium through a great number of flues near the floor, and, on the syphon principle, as fast as the vitiated air is drawn out, the warm air stored above the hall rushes down through the ceiling, which is a network

of perforations in beautiful scrollwork patterns, and takes the place of that which has been exhausted.

The whole process is accomplished so gradually that nothing like a draft is felt by the audience. The regulation of the temperature is automatic, a certain degree of warmth serving to shut off the flow of heat.

The corridors are spacious, handsome and well lighted, without being ornate, and one of them, on the balcony floor is likely to become a popular resort and a place of weird sounds, for its arched ceiling has given it a peculiar capacity for reverberation, so that a word or sentence spoken suddenly will continue to ring in the ears for 10 seconds, like that which follows the striking of a tuning fork.

There are four spacious coatrooms, two on the ground floor and two on the balcony floor, accommodating altogether more than 2000 persons, and there are reception rooms for both men and women with every attendant comfort that can be asked for.

There are two main entrances, the principal one on Huntington av, the other on Massachusetts av, and in addition there are 12 exits.

A box office is located at each main entrance, but the one which will be open all day is that on the Massachusetts av side.

The two balconies are reached by four different staircases of marble, the steps so fashioned as to be climbed with the least possible exertion, and the location of each stairway is indicated by a red light.

The sculptured and painted decorations of the hall are after the Italian renaissance style, light, airy and full of flowing grace.

From roof to cellar the building is fireproof, containing practically nothing capable of burning.

One thing is certain—while the hall retains its present form there can be no grand opera or other dramatic performance in it, for it would be utterly impossible to erect a set of scenery upon the stage as it is built.

Thomas A. Fox, who has represented the architect, Mr McKim of New York, during the erection of the building, contributed much to the pleasure of the visitors to the hall last evening by his intelligent and comprehensive description of the structure and its embellishments.

The public will have its first opportunity to see the hall on the night of the formal opening, Oct 15.

The manager, Charles A. Ellis, who had Music hall so many years, will be assisted as in the past by Fred R. Comee and Louis H. Mudgett.

The Boston Globe praises the decor and amenities of Symphony Hall, September 22, 1900.

Architecturally, Symphony Hall looks, from the outside, like nothing so much as an Italian Renaissance church of the early basilican type. Its high central gabled roof is like the roof over the nave of such a church, and it is flanked by lower side roofs like those that covered the aisles and chapels. At Symphony Hall, the "nave" is the concert hall itself, and the flanking wings serve the patrons and staff. The church form is well suited to the symphony's function: The orchestra and its conductor, at least from an architectural point of view, resemble the clergyman and his altar in the apse of a church. Unfortunately, the form of Symphony Hall ceased to express its internal order on the sad day when the main entrance, facing Huntington Avenue, had to be closed because of a street and subway underpass. Originally, visitors entered the hall as one would normally enter a church, directly on axis with the procession to the stage. A visitor would sense, subliminally, that the plan of the hall reflected the symmetry of his or her own body, with the stage as the head. Today, ducking into the mouse-hole side entrance on Massachusetts Avenue, we sense none of this. It remains to be seen whether future renovations will be able to restore a more generous and gracious entrance, one that again orients the visitor to the internal order of the building.

In detail, the building is simple: a brick box with limestone trim, the materials of much of Harvard, of the Massachusetts State House, and of many other well-known local buildings. For all its Renaissance sources, Symphony Hall retains a Bostonian look. It is a quietly handsome building. Its architecture immediately asserts a public, civic presence. It avoids novelty, originality, and display, preferring instead an unassuming, conservative, and familiar "good taste." This preference—for better or worse—remains an essential part of the Boston character today. ✑

—*Robert Campbell*

The author thanks the BSO for allowing him an early view of the manuscript of the book, The Making of Symphony Hall, Boston: A History with Documents *by Richard Poate Stebbins, without which this summary could not have been written.*

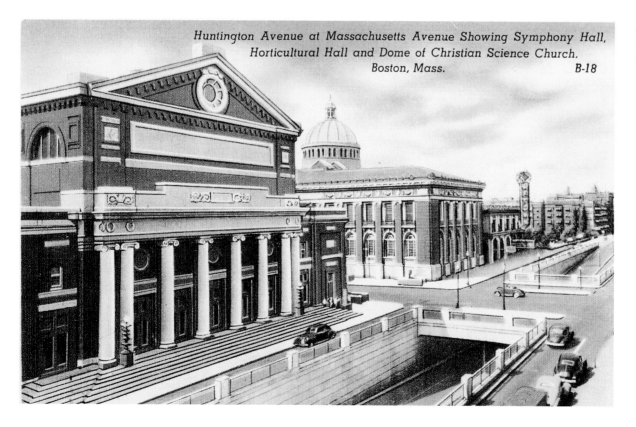

A postcard depicts the view of the hall from Huntington Avenue after the underpass was built in the early 1940s.

Paul Spencer Byard

The Genius of Symphony Hall:
A Legacy for the Future

To this admiring New Yorker, Symphony Hall at its centenary remains the most Old Boston of buildings. It starts by being very good at what it does: The hall is at heart a technical building—one of America's first—and its technical excellence is at the level of genius. It contains its genius in a big, burly body—it might once have played football—and clothes it to reflect a prejudice for austerity and thrift in brown-red brick and limestone as close as may be to old tweed. Like many other distinguished bodies near its age, the hall has a decided limp from an unfortunate accident some time ago—the suppression of Huntington Avenue that basically wrecked its public circulation. But even now the hall still carries these attributes, with a definite Boston insouciance—almost an indifference—to what you may want to make of them. As a work of art, it exists not to accommodate you but to be what it is.

This Boston combination of character and obduracy about what it is makes Symphony Hall an awesome collaborator for architects charged with perpetuating its peculiar ingenuity. What makes the collaboration still more stimulating, however, is something not just Bostonian but universal in what the hall is so resistant about, particularly when viewed at the start of the new millennium. The hall's genius, after all, is for music made in your presence by the muscular actions of humans. In the big picture of the evolution of music, this may just be a stage in an evolution of technology, like the phonograph, the last bastion of the analog. On the other hand, in the current accelerating explosion—the Big Bang, even—of the virtual, the hall and its music seem all the more valuable for what seems their reality: as the genuine thing we value not for its comfort but for its authenticity, as the measure and test of everything else.

Given its technical excellence in particular, the hall matters as one of the places where we most closely approach the meaning of the human experience; the rest is all made up to serve. Going into the new millennium, the perpetuation of this rare, sharp touchstone for the understanding of our lives is a task of exceptional importance.

This recognition of the hall's genius is not just a pleasure to be savored in the course of the renewal. Like all work with great old architecture, renewal starts with the understanding of the meaning of the human experience for which the old building is prized and of the precise ways its architecture creates and controls it. Successful design with old buildings then proceeds from this understanding, to be sure whatever is necessarily added to the old architecture enhances and celebrates that prized meaning and keeps it in control of the combined architectural outcome. The recognition of the hall's greatness—its meaning for Boston, New York, and the world—is thus the heart of the discipline that will make the renewal a success.

Understanding

Seeing Symphony Hall as a Boston building is seeing it in the light by which it was conceived. New York's Carnegie Hall predated Symphony Hall by just ten years and was Major Higginson's point of reference for almost everything he didn't want his Music Hall to be. For the form of the New York hall, Andrew Carnegie drew on New York's old Academy of Music, an operatic, tiered horseshoe that worked pretty well musically. The New York form paid considerable attention to the comforts and pleasures of its patrons and established relatively intimate connections among members of the audience as well as between the audience and its artists. Higginson was firm that he wanted something quite different, almost exactly like

his Boston precedent—the old Boston Music Hall.

Higginson was also reflecting an interesting turn of the times between the building of the two halls. Designing in the 1880s, Carnegie was rounding out an era—the Gilded Age—that valued a certain fleshy excess in its architecture, an architecture that generated a certain warmth of interaction that remains a key part of its success. Higginson may have been predisposed to reject those excesses by some Boston gene, but he was also just enough beyond their time to be in tune with other patrons also wanting to reject them, including the patrons of the great architectural correction of the World's Columbian Exposition in Chicago, in 1893. There, the assembled architects of America set out to get the nation as a whole to reject the Gilded Age by offering a powerful, bright white Beaux-Arts alternative to make all sorts of building types come out the way they thought they ought to under the different, imposing, imperial circumstances of the United States in the 1890s. Higginson had support for the difference he wanted to impose in his hall, and he had a truly great architect—Charles Follen McKim—working nearby on the Public Library and at Harvard, ready to deliver the new architecture in any form he would like it. Higginson had a site more generous than Carnegie's that—after a major false start with a different Roman form—had room for the ample, orderly, symmetrical, Beaux-Arts procession into the hall that would set up the experience he wanted to offer.

Higginson also had Wallace Sabine, something completely new under the sun. Sabine gave McKim and Higginson the calculations they needed to make their special-purpose building fit its special purpose to a standard never achieved or achievable before. There is a degree

to which, in adapting Symphony Hall so closely and scientifically to its purpose, they made it an early "modern" building. As important for architects who need to understand the hall's meaning as architecture, they also made its form and its technology crucial to its genius. It is the control of the experience leading up to the hall, and then the technical excellence of the hall itself, that in the end make sense of its austerity, giving it a reason and a rigor beyond Higginson's peculiar taste and corrective bent and creating the tool to manage the character of what is added. The austerity became part of an internal hierarchy of the hall as a work of art that subordinated everything to the experience of music and the perfection of the sound.

Neither Carnegie Hall nor Symphony Hall ever, strictly speaking, had a problem with its sound. But they both had severe and parallel problems with the whole apparatus that supported making their sounds, as that apparatus evolved from the assumptions about it built into their original buildings. Higginson's administrative assumptions, for example, were simple: he would run the place himself. All he needed was an office and a desk. He would run it with funds of his own and from friends and with income earned from the music itself, including the Pops he so ingeniously invented and built into the hall's architecture. Andrew Carnegie's revenue assumptions were less inventive—he originally offered "Lodge Rooms" tucked in the roof trusses for rent to Masons—and they crumbled more quickly under the relatively brutal pressures on the arts in New York. The realities of those pressures came home when, after World War II, the New York Philharmonic decided to leave Carnegie Hall and move to Lincoln Center.

That move was, of course, very nearly curtains for Carnegie: The red-checked tower cheerfully offered in

A view of the auditorium from the second balcony; enthusiastic applause from both balconies, c. 1950

Life as a replacement remains one of the iconic images of the crisis of the 1960s and '70s—the reaction against public innovation—that eventually brought us the twentieth century's intensely conservative last quarter. The brush with death made acute for Carnegie what in fact affected both halls: the need to improve physical conditions for every one of the participants in its music-making— musicians, audiences, patrons, and administrators—at a time when pleasing them was getting harder all the time. Both halls were facing what would soon have been a century of rising expectations concerning the circumstances in which it was reasonable to expect the participants to make their contributions to the act of making music. The need was intensified by the impacts of the same passage of time on music, as serious art music exploded beyond the relatively comfortable conventions of tonality and time, making the presentation and absorption of its insights much, much harder work for everyone.

Renewal
At the time the present renewal began in the early 1980s, both halls were worn—Boston shabby, Carnegie worn through in many places—and both halls lacked space for the functions that had come to be essential to the whole expanded enterprise of music-making. Most important, both were hobbled by disabilities at the heart of their organization as architecture: in the public circulation systems that tied all parts of the buildings together around the public sequence into the music rooms from the street. Boston's circulation problem was in part a problem of rising expectations—you really couldn't expect late-twentieth-century audiences to pack in up the steps like the crowds for rush tickets in the famous painting. But with the crippling Act of Public Authority of the construction of the Huntington Avenue underpass, the problem became a real physical handicap. Higginson's front door became, effectively, inaccessible. Gone with it was McKim's logical, generous, Beaux-Arts progression from Huntington Avenue into the lobby, with symmetrical corridors and stairs on both

sides. Gone was one of the paramount purposes of Higginson's strong, controlling, symmetrical architecture: to set its patrons up for the serious experience inside. Fixed instead was the awkward, lopsided crush from Massachusetts Avenue into one side of the hall, which has been part of the Boston concert-going experience ever since.

Carnegie's circulation was not a problem of Higginsonian principle, but the fact that the long slog of its vertical stacking was increasingly unacceptable to patrons, particularly without an elevator and particularly when coupled with a tiny, jammed lobby that was little more than a landing on its long stairs. The architects of Carnegie's renewal, James Stewart Polshek & Partners, found an answer by dropping the lobby to the level of the street and reworking the stairs and box office around it. The rest of Carnegie's plan fell into place around this change. With its eye on Carnegie's plan and a sense of its success with issues it also needed to address, the Boston Symphony then retained Carnegie's architects to prepare a similar master plan for

Symphony Hall. The crucial insight of the architects' resulting plan for the hall once again had to do with entry and circulation. After considerable study, the plan concluded that Huntington Avenue could never be completely redeemed as a worthy principal entry, either by way of the original entry or by way of a parallel entry farther down Huntington Avenue through the Cohen Wing. Nothing short of an unlikely second Big Dig could sufficiently relieve the constrictions at the intersection of Massachusetts and Huntington avenues to resurrect McKim's and Higginson's intended direct and generous entry sequence from the south.

It did occur to the architects, however, that the experience might be substantially restored if the old circulation system could be entirely reversed to start from the north—if a new generous lobby could be provided at the middle of the back of the hall, with new passages on both sides leading symmetrically under the wings of the stage and into the hall through the original corridors. Given the height of the stage, and with a little additional tinkering with grades to lower the new lobby a foot or so below the existing grade, there would in fact be room to pass under the stage wings.

This new lobby would have a number of happy consequences. Since the new entries would pass under the stage wings, the hall's minuscule sidestage spaces could be vastly expanded, particularly toward the west, with a level connection to a new Musician's Wing in the parking lot providing badly needed tuning, dressing, and other spaces intended to improve the lives of the Symphony's musicians. Within the hall, the old Huntington Avenue entry, the Hatch Room, and the Cabot-Cahners Room above it could shed some of their ambiguity as sort-of circulation, sort-of reception, spaces and become the whole-hearted and relatively noble patron spaces their architecture still calls out for them to become. The Cohen Wing, finally, would be properly situated down the architectural hierarchy from the entry and the hall itself, in a good position to provide the support services to which, as a

fairly humble structure, its architecture was inherently best adapted.

The move would have major architectural consequences for the hall as a whole. It would put the entry directly at the bend in Massachusetts Avenue behind the hall, where most patrons in fact arrive from the prime sources of parking. It would create the opportunity for an architectural event at that same bend in Massachusetts Avenue where Symphony Hall principally shows itself off to the city, across from the First Church of Christ, Scientist. The addition might include a new performance and event space that could, among many other things, give the old plan of the hall new resemblances to the plans of its great ancestors, the Leipzig Gewandhaus and the Concertgebouw, in Amsterdam. And the addition could announce the renewal at an important place in the city with an adventurous form that grew out of the form of the hall and allowed the old form to remain in control of the very bold fact of having been turned back-to-front.

In the immediate next years, the Symphony completed the first phase of the Master Plan to improve service spaces and patron facilities in what became the Cohen Wing. At the same time, attending to very different, uniquely Boston business, they had the Polshek office prepare the conceptual design for the rustic, open-ended shoebox that later emerged as Ozawa Hall at Tanglewood. Carnegie finished its centennial renewal: The new lobby, circulation, and service systems were a huge blessing, and the renovation as a whole did everything intended for Carnegie Hall as an institution. The Boston Symphony had a comparable success as Ozawa Hall consolidated and enriched the contributions of Tanglewood to its musical and institutional life. The Symphony then retained Anne Beha Associates as architects to study and make a number of careful changes in the hall—some in the perimeter, and some delicate and very successful ones in the hall itself—to rationalize and improve its lighting, leaving the room much cleaner, brighter, and more serene. As the Centennial

approached, the Symphony added Platt Byard Dovell Architects of New York to the team, asking them all to look afresh at the issues underlying the old Master Plan to see what might work now.

The issues remained basically what they had been, only intensified in certain respects by the passage of time. At the top of the hierarchy was the marvelous music room itself: not that it should be changed in any way, but whether the balance of its amenity—the intensity of its native severity—might somehow be lightened up to make it just a touch cheerier and inviting for new audiences. At a minimum, the matter might be as simple as reactivating the hall's built-in access to natural light. Like the windows of its great ancestors, the hall's long-painted-over windows could offer its audiences a kind of contact with the outside world even as they listened—an attribute that originally distinguished the experience of music from that of theater—and might reintroduce the wide color spectrum of natural light to bring more life to colors like McKim's. Given the continued presence of shutters—the old ones, plus some of the original pulleys, were still there—the light, of course, could be used only when truly helpful.

Crucial among the issues overall was still the proper accommodation of the musicians: suitable lockers, practice, tuning, and preparation spaces and, for the first time in a hundred years, ready level access to the stage. And largest among the issues remained the needs of patrons, both how to improve access, entry, and circulation for them and how to provide suitable space for all the events related to concerts that have become

so important to their support. What architectural form the result would take would depend on the inherent requirements of the needed spaces, but, just as important, on the way they would be added to the hall to build on and support its purposes. The architecture needed to grow from the hall, evolve from and extend the logic of Higginson's landmark, the addition making itself part of a larger whole with the old building, even while differing from it as much as it had to in its own expression to reflect its times and its own very different reality. Meeting these needs and setting up a worthy combined work of architecture celebrating and extending the genius of the hall was the happy challenge once again in the hands of the Master Plan architects.

Caroline Smedvig

Casts of Character:
The Symphony Statues

Stare out into the vastness of an empty Symphony Hall. Who stares back? A satyr—a dancing one—as well as Sophocles, Euripides, Demosthenes, and Apollo.

These "casts of character" are among the sixteen mythological deities and legendary figures of antiquity who continually survey Symphony Hall. Striking elegantly languid poses from their second-balcony niches, they surely have the best "seats" in the house. These statues—all plaster casts of Old World originals—have been ensconced in their niches since the early 1900s, when a generous group of Symphony Friends selected and donated them to the hall.

The idea for the statues originated with the hall's architects, McKim, Mead & White, and its acoustical adviser, Wallace C. Sabine. Sabine saw the statuary as the solution to two problems confronting them at the time: The beautiful casts could embellish large wall surfaces in the hall while providing places where acoustical adjustments could be made. If the hall's acoustics needed to be altered, fabric or felt could be placed behind the statues without disturbing the decor. As it turned out, Symphony Hall was so masterfully designed that it was never necessary to change the acoustics in a significant way.

Florence Wolsky, although semiretired, is a member of the Museum of Fine Arts Ancient Arts Department and one of the original Symphony Hall tour guides. Mrs. Wolsky has thoroughly researched the statues and their history. After more than thirty years of familiarity, her passion and affection for them remain undimmed.

The use of reproductions, explains Mrs. Wolsky, was extremely popular in the nineteenth century. At the

Paris Exposition of 1867, a resolution was passed that everyone in the world had the right to be exposed to quality reproductions of the great statues of Greece and Rome.

Mrs. Wolsky explains: "There were very strong feelings of cultural uplift at the time, much the same feeling that was behind Major Higginson's impulse to found the Boston Symphony after he had traveled to Europe, had heard the great symphonies there, and seen the great art. People in Boston had a strong desire to bring great art to this country, since they believed it brought out the noblest instincts in man, and therefore created a better democracy."

"Since most Greek sculpture was rendered in bronze, not marble, most statuary was melted down. The Romans, however, adored Greek sculpture, and made numerous copies, in marble, of Greek statues, which have survived."

Roman marbles, like their Greek predecessors, were rarely available for purchase. As a result, American specialists like Pietro Caproni and his brother—whose studios were at the corner of Washington and Newcomb streets in Roxbury—traveled to Europe, copying the originals with precision, grace, and plaster.

According to Mrs. Wolsky, the actual selection of the Caproni plaster casts was entrusted to Mrs. John W. Elliot and a committee of about two hundred Friends of Symphony. The group pored over the Caproni brothers' catalogues, eventually choosing the sixteen statues now in the hall.

These statues were an appropriate addition to the neoclassical design of Symphony Hall, since the ancient Romans often decorated their odeons or theaters with such objects of art. The Caproni casts were not in place for the hall's opening concert, but were added one at a time as they

emerged from Caproni's studios. These statues, in Mrs. Wolsky's opinion, may well have been chosen with an eye toward beauty, as well as for their relevance to music, art, literature, and oratory. Two of the statues depict Apollo, the god of music and poetry. The first—set second from the right, as you face the stage—is known as *Apollo Citharodeus*. Copied from the original in the Palazzo dei Conservatori in Rome and based on a Greek statue from about 430 B.C., it shows Apollo in the long robes of a musician. He is accompanying his songs and poetry on a cithara, an instrument similar to a lyre he is credited with inventing. On his head is a laurel wreath—the symbol of triumph in Greece and Rome—which was given to victors in the games and contests sacred to Apollo.

The second statue of Apollo—to the right, as you face the back of the hall—is the *Apollo Belvedere*, credited for generations as the highest ideal of male beauty. The original, in the Vatican Museum, is thought to be a Roman copy of a fourth-century work by Leochares, the court sculptor to Alexander the Great. Here, Apollo is shown as a divine hero, wearing a chlamys, or short cloak, and holding a bow in his left hand. A spray of the sacred laurel plant may once have rested in his other

hand. A creature of earth and the underworld, the snake, is coiled around the tree stump, symbolizing Apollo's role as a god of prophecy.

To the left of this statue stands Diana of Versailles, currently in the Louvre and also a copy of a fourth-century work by Leochares. Diana—known to the Greeks as Artemis, goddess of the chase and the forests—is shown here in the woods, flanked by a small stag. Wearing her hunting costume, a short tunic, she once readied a bow in her left hand. Like her brother, Apollo, Diana was a musician who often led her choir of muses and graces at Delphi on returning from the hunt.

Three statues represent satyrs, or fauns—mythological creatures human in form, with the ears and tail of a goat. Satyrs were followers of Dionysus, the god of drama and music. The first satyr—first to the right, as you face the stage—has the infant Bacchus, or Dionysus, riding on his shoulders, grasping a bunch of grapes. The satyr holds a pair of cymbals. On the stump beside him is a panther skin, sacred to Dionysus, as well as Pan-pipes, grapes, and vine leaves.

The second satyr—fourth on the right, facing the stage—is known as

buried by the eruption of Mount Vesuvius in 79 A.D. and listed in an old Caprini Catalogue as Mnemosyne, Mother of the Muses.

As beautiful as they are, the statues of Symphony Hall have not always been hailed as noble additions to the architecture. Since their installation, letters and comments have been registered from concertgoers concerned with the statues' state of dishabille. As recently as 1947, one gentleman wrote to the former board president Henry B. Cabot:

I dare say no two cocktail bars in Boston are as seductive a medium and raise so much havoc with virgins as does Symphony Hall by means of its suggestive display of male privates.... Symphony Hall is one of the remaining symbols of Boston culture. Let us keep it serene. I do not know how art would be affected if the privates on the statues should be covered. All these figures have some sort of scarf about the shoulders, might it not be brought down lower?

Responded Mr. Cabot:

I am afraid that were we to take your advice, somebody might quote to us a stanza from the old rhyme by Anthony Comstock which, as I remember, is:

So keep your temper, Anthony.
Don't mind the people's roars.
We'll drape the tables' dainty legs
In cotton flannel drawers.
We'll cover all those nudities
That your pure nature fret,
And put a bustle on the nag
To hide her red rosette.

Above, far left, left to right:
Faun with Infant Bacchus,
Apollo Citharoedus,
Mnemosyne, Mother of the Muses;
above, from lower left, clockwise:
Seated Anacreon,
Diana of Versailles,
Apollo Citharoedus,
Sophocles

The Dancing Faun. The original is currently in the Villa Borghese in Rome. This satyr, older and bearded, plays the cymbals while dancing, as he would in a procession honoring Dionysus. Another panther skin is draped on the stump behind him, his body twisted in the vigorous "contrapposto" typical of late Hellenistic art.

The third satyr—first on the left, as you face the stage—originated with Praxiteles, one of the three greatest sculptors of the fourth century A.D. As Mrs. Wolsky points out, Praxiteles was a virtuoso in stone sculpture and gave marble a translucent, soft surface that conveys the impression of human skin. A marvelous example of the characteristic grace of a Praxitelean statue, this one shows a languid, dreamy satyr leaning against a tree stump. It is often called *The Marble Faun*, from the book by Nathaniel Hawthorne it reportedly inspired.

Also represented in Symphony Hall are Demosthenes (fifth from the right as you face the stage); two statues of the Greek poet Anacreon (sixth from the right and fifth from the left); Euripides (seventh from the right); Hermes (third from the left); Athena (fourth from the left); Sophocles (fifth from the left); and the Greek orator Aeschines (seventh from the left).

One statue that has an indirect connection to the arts, at best, is that of the Amazon (second from the left), thought to be a copy of a fifth-century work by Polycleitus. The Amazon was probably chosen since it is one of the most famous statues of antiquity. Amazons were followers of the musician Diana. Mrs. Wolsky suspects that there may have been a desire to represent another woman in the statuary, in addition to Diana, Athena, and the so-called Woman from Herculaneum (third from the right), one of the statues

Under the sign of Beethoven

Symphony Hall was built, quite literally, under the sign of Beethoven, for it is his name in the central shield at the top of the stage proscenium. The other plaques on the sides of the arch remain blank. Having only Beethoven's name can be seen from two perspectives. One is that Beethoven, a challenger of tradition and destroyer of old form and the most influential symphonic composer of all, would never be surpassed by anyone coming later. But Henry Lee Higginson also implicitly recognized that the future might well bring significant new composers and new musical approaches.

In its nineteen seasons before the opening of Symphony Hall, the Boston Symphony strongly focused on symphonic repertoire that fit solidly in the tradition of Beethoven. Higginson's only programming request of its first music director, Georg Henschel (1850-1934), was that the first season feature all nine Beethoven symphonies (although only the first three movements of the Ninth were performed). German-Austrian music—Beethoven's in particular, but also that of living composers such as Brahms and Strauss—dominated the repertory. The German conductors that Higginson hired in the Symphony's first decades—Henschel, Wilhelm Gericke (1845-1925), Arthur Nikisch (1855-1922), and Emil Paur (1855-1932)—were, after all, personally acquainted with many of the eminent German composers of the day. Once in Boston, they began to program as well the music of their new composer-colleagues in New England, including that of Mrs. H. H. A. Beach, Edward MacDowell, and George Chadwick. This connection to American music quickly became one of the pillars of the Boston Symphony tradition, becoming particularly important during the later tenure of Serge Koussevitzky.

Wilhelm Gericke, then in his second term as conductor, led the BSO in its first few seasons in the new Symphony Hall. Responding to criticism, he began to update his repertory by performing less familiar compositions, introducing the music of Elgar, d'Indy, and Glazunov as well as conducting American premieres of such works as Bruckner's Fifth Symphony and Bruch's Serenade in A minor for violin and orchestra. In 1906, after a contract dispute with Higginson, Gericke was replaced by another German, Karl Muck (1859-1940), who came to Boston from the Royal Opera House in Berlin with the highest credentials of any BSO conductor up to that time. The Kaiser had released Muck temporarily from his position at the Opera House, so his first term was for only two years. But the effect of his work with the orchestra on both players and public was so positive that every effort was expended to bring him back as soon as possible. Muck was famous for

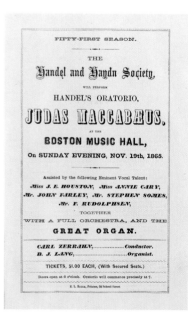

Above, The Boston Symphony Orchestra in 1882 in Boston Music Hall, Georg Henschel (1850-1934), conductor; near right, a Handel & Haydn Society program from a performance in Boston Music Hall; far right, the program from the inaugural concert with the antiquated spelling of Missa Solemnis

The first four BSO conductors: Georg Henschel (1850-1934), the first conductor, served for three years; Wilhelm Gericke (1845-1925) held the post twice—first for five seasons and as the fifth conductor for eight years; Arthur Nikisch (1855-1922), conductor for four seasons; and Emil Paur (1855-1932), for five seasons.

his performances of Wagner, and he introduced Schoenberg (his Five Pieces for Orchestra, Op. 16) into the BSO repertory, but he was also receptive to the new stylistic winds blowing in France, and, in 1907, he led the American premiere of Debussy's epochal work, *La Mer.*

Muck himself suggested his (as it turned out, interim) replacement, the German Max Fiedler (1859-1939)—no relation to the celebrated Arthur. Like his predecessors, Fiedler attempted to balance the classics (which by this time included Brahms and Wagner) with the modern. He led the first BSO performance of Bruckner's Eighth Symphony and the first music by the Englishman Frederick Delius to be heard in Symphony Hall. However well Fiedler did his job, though, he was always under the shadow of the enormous enthusiasm that Muck had generated.

Karl Muck returned to Boston in 1912 and, three years later, took the orchestra on its first transcontinental trip, giving thirteen concerts at the Panama-Pacific Exposition in San Francisco. In

1917, the Symphony made its first recordings, for RCA. But with a world war raging in Europe, anti-German fever was increasing in the United States; at its height Muck was ignominiously arrested and confined as an enemy alien in the last months of the war.

POSTWAR, POST-HIGGINSON, POST-GERMAN

Muck's arrest was not simply a personal catastrophe for the conductor but also marked a major change in the character of the orchestra itself. The originally "German" orchestra had already begun to yield to a more international style under the direction of Muck, who, it was reported, supported the tendency to find French players for the woodwinds, Germans for the brass sections, and Austrians and Americans for the strings. But, until 1918, the conductor whose sensibility shaped all of these players into a musical whole had always represented a Germanic school of music-making.

Higginson was himself aging and ill, and it seemed to him that his life's work was in danger of collapsing under the weight of the political passions of wartime. Clearly, the next conductor of the Boston Symphony could not be German. He had already made two fruitless attempts to entice Sergei Rachmaninoff to Boston, but now there was not only the fear of Germany but also the "Red scare" brought on by the Russian Revolution. Only France was left—at least in the mind of Higginson, who always felt that anyone from Europe would be preferable to an American (or so George Chadwick commented bitterly in his private family memoir).

Karl Muck (1859-1940), a two-term conductor of the BSO who was interned as an enemy alien in 1918; at right, Boston Symphony Orchestra Brass Choir during the 1921-1922 season

The Brass Choir · Boston Symphony Orchestra

Everett Firth

A View from the Stage

I have spent most of my life, and all of my musical life, within the confines of Symphony Hall. It is simply the finest hall in the world in which to create great music.

Since my instruments (timpani) remain onstage at all times, any maintenance work, changing of heads, or practicing must be accomplished onstage. To perform on this stage is to bask in acoustics like warmth from the sun. The quality of sound emanating from my colleagues can be overwhelmingly beautiful, passionate, rich, and exciting beyond words.

Even to this day, as I step onto that stage when the hall is lit but empty, the ambiance is awesome. It has a sombering greatness that defies description. When you consider all the great professionals—conductors, composers, soloists, orchestra players—who have made music in this temple, it brings shivers to your spine. The nobility of the air raises your head. If only the walls, the statues, the seats, would testify to what they have witnessed: the sounds, the temperament, the moods, the great artistry.

From my first concert to the present day, the thrill and ecstasy of the music have only increased with my knowledge of the music. I consider myself extremely fortunate for having spent my musical life in this, the world's greatest temple of music.

Everett Firth, c. 1999, member of the Boston Symphony Orchestra since 1952

String Choir Principals...Boston Symphony Orchestra.

Max Fiedler (1859-1939), conductor, 1908-1912; at left, the String Choir principals of the BSO during the 1923-1924 season

So the great change took place: From being a German orchestra under a German conductor, the Boston Symphony became more of a French orchestra under a French conductor. Higginson, now eighty-four, decided in February of 1918 that it was time for him to let go the reins. He brought together nine prominent Bostonians who would become trustees upon the incorporation of the orchestra and who would assure its continuation. The operating manager, Charles A. Ellis, who had held that position since the first season, also chose to retire at that time, and soon afterward Muck was arrested. At one stroke, the three leaders of the Boston Symphony—financial, administrative, and artistic—were gone.

It was a dangerous time for the continuation of the orchestra, but the biggest problem of all was finding a worthy conductor on short notice. After many cables and with the new season only weeks away, the French composer Henri Rabaud (1873-1949)—whose *Marouf* had just been staged by New York's Metropolitan Opera—accepted the position. Rabaud could not make it for the opening of the season, so the first concerts were conducted by a Frenchman then working at the Metropolitan Opera, Pierre Monteux (1875-1964). Rabaud arrived at last and led a season dominated by the sturdy familiarity of Beethoven, the elegance of Saint-Saëns, and the exotic brilliance of Rimsky-Korsakov. There was no Wagner and only a little Brahms. But Rabaud was really more interested in composing than in conducting, and after one year he returned to France.

This time, the choice of a successor was easy; the orchestra had already found a conductor to its taste. Pierre Monteux had brought together a demoralized group and made it perform with much of its old glory. An even larger challenge lay ahead: Monteux was in charge on the one

A large flag hung in front of the hall in 1917 was intended to express patriotism after the BSO was accused of unpatriotic behavior due to its association with Karl Muck.

Stephen Jay Gould
The Soul of a City

What makes a city great? For urbanophiles like myself, no question can be more important, or more difficult, to answer. We can agree that however many may be called, few are chosen. (One might make a case for Philadelphia, New Orleans, and others, but only four cities clearly occupy this rank in the United States: Boston, Chicago, New York, and San Francisco—in alphabetical order to avoid further arguments.) We might also achieve consensus about a few prerequisites: distinctiveness, walkability (the key point that Europeans understand and Americans often do not), safety, aesthetics, and diversity of neighborhoods.

As an evolutionary biologist with an ineradicable affection for history, I would also add continuity of historical traditions to the list, for a great city must grow into its status and cannot be created *ex nihilo* (the utopian fallacy). Continuity, however, may surpass all other criteria in stringency, for its achievement must walk a fine line between stodgy ossification on one side (Boston's problem, happily now overcome, when I first moved here in the late 1960s) and the rootlessness of successive blitzkriegs to pristine "renewal" on the other.

This continuity requires both personal and architectural inputs: the energy of passionate and truly urbane people (literally, devoted to the urbs, or city) and the stability ensured by great places. If we ask how places achieve the depth and vitality of greatness—while avoiding decay and desuetude—I would venture three main routes (one best exemplified by Symphony Hall, which I have not forgotten, despite the verbosity of this prologue). Irrelevancy and stodginess can be fended off, first, by capturing something so universal and so moving that the passage of time cannot dim the impact. In this category, for

Boston, I nominate the pride and determination on the faces of the first black soldiers in the Civil War, as sculpted by Augustus Saint-Gaudens in bas-relief on the Boston Common, just across from the State House. Second, a great place may hold vibrancy by self-renewal. Here, I nominate the magnolia trees of Commonwealth Avenue and those glorious few days, repeated each year, of their full bloom.

Third, a fixed place, however eminent in setting or architecture, may achieve greatness by maintaining a noble purpose, continued in each generation by new people of fierce commitment and equal but different excellence. Here, Boston boasts two spectacular examples: Symphony Hall and Fenway Park—a comparison that may strike some snobbish people as sacrilegious but that most sensible and ecumenical Bostonians will recognize and cherish.

Ruth, Williams, Martinez, as three generations of baseball supremacy in America's finest park, opened in 1912. Koussevitsky, Munch, and Ozawa, as three conductors, each at the pinnacle of a different style of excellence, in America's finest (and most acoustically rewarding) concert hall, opened in 1900. Can anyone fail to rank these two continuities of superb performance—housed, without any break in genealogy, in two of Boston's finest and most distinctive buildings—as a key ingredient in the greatness of a city that, without such a rich history and such continuity in varied excellence, might be deemed a bit too small to occupy this highest rank of merit?

Finally, and as a million other people could easily testify, such a strong affection for Symphony Hall, evoking a feeling that knows no other word than "love," must be nurtured by a personal bond of experience, not only by abstract appreciation. Everyone's testimony will be

different—for such is the cumulative strength of variety in true excellence. Let me make my idiosyncratic summary by noting that the building and its foremost institution moved me most powerfully on two occasions, representing both the softest and the loudest moments in the entire classical repertory.

First, as a young man new to Boston some thirty years ago, I bought the last available seat in the back row of the upper balcony to hear Dietrich Fischer-Dieskau sing Schubert's great song cycle, *Die Schöne Müllerin.* My spine tingled as the utter beauty and pure intensity of his triple pianissimos reached my seat without the slightest diminution. Now, I said to myself, I understand what they mean by "perfect" acoustics!

Second, at the other end, I sang in a performance of Berlioz's Requiem (as a member of the Boston Cecilia, recruited to augment the Tanglewood Chorus for this most massive of all choral works) under Ozawa and the BSO one summer at Tanglewood. I knew the piece well, from listening to recordings and performances, but had never experienced its grandeur from the inside. During the first rehearsal with full orchestra, at the loudest moment when the four supplementary brass choirs finally amalgamate to their climax and as the row of I-don't-know-how-many timpani bang out their reinforcement—all to announce the trumpet call of the Last Judgment, when the basses alone (my choral home) must ring out their *Tuba mirum* above the orchestral din—well, I just devolved into tears and spinal shivers. I had never heard such a musical racket, or felt one for that matter (as the rumble of timpani literally rose through the wooden risers and up my legs). I recovered for the performance, but I couldn't sing a note at this dress rehearsal!

Yes, such honorable continuity feeds our intellect and our emotions. The Boston Cecilia sang in the inaugural concert of Symphony Hall in 1900, presenting Beethoven's momentous *Missa Solemnis.* In October 2000, as part of the centennial season, the Boston Cecilia will join the Handel & Haydn Society to perform Mendelssohn's *Elijah* (and I shall finally fulfill my secret wish to sing in Symphony Hall)—one hundred years to the day after the same Handel & Haydn Society followed the same Boston Cecilia in Symphony Hall's opening month by singing the same great work. Can anyone suggest a better symbol or realization of continuity?

One cannot possibly quantify the sum total of beauty that has emerged from Symphony Hall throughout a century. I once wrote that if we could bottle the mental power contained in the correct spelling of horrendously complicated dinosaur names by legions of American six-year-olds, then we could truly move mountains (or complete the Big Dig in a moment). I feel the same way about the totality of beauty produced in Symphony Hall.

So let me simply cite Proverbs 3:15. We can't specify a measure, but we surely know that "she is more precious than rubies; and all the things that thou canst desire are not to be compared unto her." The very next statement (Proverbs 3:16) will also serve as a fitting tribute to continuity at the outset of a second century: "length of days is in her right hand."

occasion when musicians of the Boston Symphony went on strike. The concertmaster, Frederick Fradkin, who had some disagreement with Monteux, refused to rise with the rest of the orchestra to accept the audience's applause for a performance of Berlioz's *Symphonie fantastique*. The insult was so pointed that Fradkin was relieved of his duties. Disaffected members of the orchestra raised the question of a walkout, and thirty-six players actually refused to appear at the next performance—which meant canceling the Berlioz and substituting an unrehearsed program.

Ultimately, five of the strikers reconsidered their action and returned to the orchestra, but the others left. Monteux had to hire about a third of an orchestra immediately and train it to the stan-

Left to right, the French composer Henri Rabaud (1873-1949), the BSO's conductor for the 1918-1919 season; Pierre Monteux (1875-1964), conductor, 1919-1924; Richard Burgin, concertmaster for 42 years and assistant conductor under Monteux, Koussevitzky, and Munch; Serge Koussevitzky, (1874-1951) c. 1924

dards for which the Boston Symphony was renowned. Part of the season was lost, but he was able to end the season with a performance of the Berlioz at the accustomed level of finesse. By the fall of 1920, Monteux had made his most important appointment, that of a young violinist named Richard Burgin as concertmaster. Burgin held that position for more than forty years and played a significant role on the podium as assistant conductor through the leadership of Monteux, Koussevitzky, and Munch.

In addition to helping change the tonal complexion of the BSO from "German" to "French," Monteux was strongly interested in the newest music; he had made his early reputation conducting the premieres of ballets by Stravinsky, Debussy, and Ravel. Other conductors had been happy to play novelties regularly, but Monteux not only increased their number but also increased the stylistic challenge to the musicians and the audience. The list of composers whose work he introduced to the repertoire is probably second only to that of Koussevitzky, yet his term of office was only one fourth as long. From England he brought works of Bax, Vaughan Williams, Bliss, Holst, and others; from Italy, Respighi, Malipiero, and Casella; from Russia, Mussorgsky and, especially, Stravinsky (only his small early piece, *Fireworks*, had been played by the orchestra before Monteux's arrival); from Spain, Falla, Albeniz, and Turina; from France, Honegger, Milhaud, Roussel, and the later works of Ravel and Debussy; and from the United States, he continued to perform Carpenter, Loeffler, Hill, Chadwick, Converse, and Griffes, among others. It is probably safe to say that Monteux's extraordinary work, both in building the orchestra and in his artistic programming, laid an essential foundation for the work of Serge Koussevitzky, whose tenure would not only shape the future of the Boston Symphony but also have a profound impact on music history in the United States.

Trained in Russia, but working in France after the outbreak of the revolution, Koussevitzky (1874-1951) arrived in Boston as a representative of the two "modern" schools—Russian and French—but with a profound respect and passion for the more traditional German school. What's more, he was passionate to find American music to champion. For the encouragement of American music, in particular, and as part of his general encouragement of new music, Koussevitzky's term with the orchestra has never been surpassed: He led an average of seven premieres every year for all of his twenty-five seasons. (This evaluation does not take into account

The Boston Symphony Orchestra
with Serge Koussevitzky

A FULL RANGE OF PERFORMERS

Symphony Hall's acclaimed acoustics and sightlines make it a favorite for musicians the world over.
A veritable "who's who" of the classical music world has performed in the hall, as well as leading jazz
musicians, choral groups, and opera singers. Adding to the rich musical history of the building, The Handel &
Haydn Society has performed in Symphony Hall since 1900, and the Celebrity Series—originally called the
Aaron Richmond Concerts, after its founder—has presented distinguished artists in the hall since 1938.

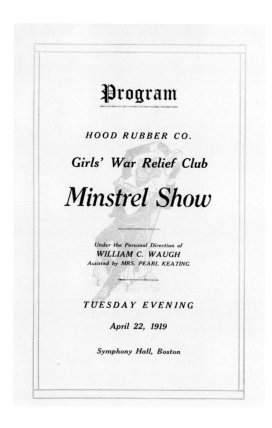

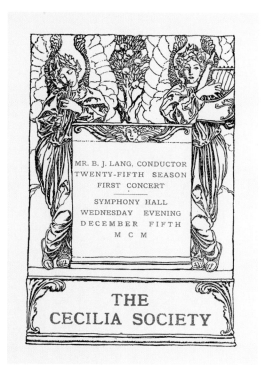

GERALDINE FARRAR
HER PHOTO DRAMATIC DEBUT IN
"CARMEN"

BOSTON SYMPHONY HALL

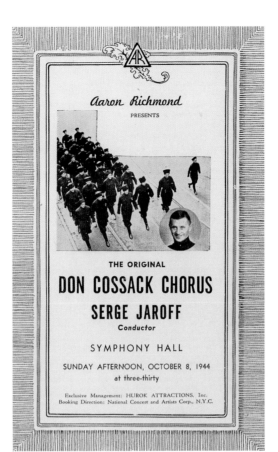

Aaron Richmond
PRESENTS

THE ORIGINAL
DON COSSACK CHORUS

SERGE JAROFF
Conductor

SYMPHONY HALL

SUNDAY AFTERNOON, OCTOBER 8, 1944
at three-thirty

Exclusive Management: HUROK ATTRACTIONS, Inc.
Booking Direction: National Concert and Artists Corp., N.Y.C.

Spike Jones
AND HIS CITY SLICKERS

★ SOUVENIR PROGRAM ★

Souvenir Program

**DUKE
Ellington
Concert**

SYMPHONY HALL
THURS. JAN. 28

net proceeds to Soldiers & Sailors fund

SYMPHONY HALL

THREE PERFORMANCES ONLY

Friday Afternoon, Nov. 5, at 2.30
Friday and Saturday Evenings, Nov. 5-6, at 8.15
THREE DIFFERENT PROGRAMMES

Mlle. ANNA
PAVLOWA
*The Incomparable
and her*
BALLET RUSSE

*Entire Drury
Lane London
organization*
in NEW BALLETS
DIVERTISSEMENTS
and OLD FAVORITE
CREATIONS
SYMPHONY
ORCHESTRA

TRIUMPHAL RETURN
TO AMERICA

ALEXANDRE
VOLININE
IVAN CLUSTINE
Maitre de Ballet
Theodore Stier
Conductor

FORTUNE GALLO, Director
Local Management:
S. HUROK, 47 West 47th Street, New York, and
L. H. MUDGETT, Symphony Hall

Koussevitzky's creation and fostering of Tanglewood, both as the summer home of the orchestra and as a significant center for training the most promising young musicians.)

Coming to the United States from France, Koussevitzky had met Americans who were studying there, particularly the students of his friend Nadia Boulanger. The first of these was Aaron Copland, whose music Koussevitzky began to promote from the beginning of his term. He conducted several early world premieres: *Music for the Theater,* in 1925, the Piano Concerto, in 1927, and Two Pieces for String Orchestra, in 1928. As Copland became well known and no longer needed Koussevitzky's patronage and support, the conductor moved on to other composers; still, he always retained a confidence in Copland's own generous recommendation of other composers whose work deserved attention. Between them, the composer and the conductor played a central role in establishing a new school of American composition and bringing it to the attention of an American audience—and, gradually, to the rest of the world.

In addition to Copland, Koussevitzky's enthusiasm for American composers led to premieres from Howard Hanson, Roy Harris, Roger Sessions, Edward Burlingame Hill, Walter Piston, William Schuman, Samuel Barber, Nikolai Berezowsky, Lukas Foss, David Diamond, Irving Fine, Vladimir Dukelsky (later known as Vernon Duke), John Alden Carpenter, Mario Castelnuovo-Tedesco, Arthur Lourié, Ernst Toch, Harold Shapero, and Leonard Bernstein, among others.

Koussevitzky recognized no geographical restriction to the creative spirit. In the first half of his Boston period, he returned to Europe every summer to attend festivals of new music, seeking works to bring to Boston. This approach had the advantage of his having heard the music in per-

Many distinguished artists have performed at Symphony Hall, both with the Boston Symphony Orchestra and in recital. Left to right, Yehudi Menuhin first performed a solo recital in 1931. Composer Aaron Copland's first work performed in the hall was his Music for the Theatre *on November 20, 1925. Artur Rubinstein performed in Symphony Hall as early as in 1920. Jascha Heifetz first performed in the hall in 1918.*

At right, season highlights in the Boston Herald, *September 1936*

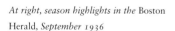

formance. Commissions, however essential for generating new music, are always a problem: the result is somewhat unpredictable. Koussevitzky combined both approaches with notable success, generating an extraordinary group of works of which a considerable share has joined the active repertory, and much of the rest still deserves performance and occasional reconsideration.

Among the foreign composers who had premieres under his baton, we find Arnold Bax, Arthur Bliss, Alfredo Casella, Manuel de Falla, Camargo Guarnieri, Arthur Honegger, Paul Hindemith, Jacques Ibert, Gian Francesco Malipiero, Igor Markevitch, Bohuslav Martinů, Olivier Messiaen, Darius Milhaud, Albert Roussel, Ottorino Respighi, Sergei Prokofiev, Béla Bartók, Benjamin Britten, Jean Sibelius, Dmitri Shostakovich, Nikolai Tcherepnin, Heitor Villa-Lobos, Alexander Tansman, Germaine Tailleferre, and Karol Szymanowski.

Symphony Soloists Prepare for Season

MYRA HESS, foremost woman pianist, spent the summer months at her home in England, preparing for her American concert tour. She will be one of the soloists during the coming Symphony season which begins October 9. (Annie Friedberg)

ALBERT SPALDING, violinist, with his dogs at his summer home at Great Barrington, in the Berkshires. (Cosmo Sileo)

RUTH POSSELT, Medford girl who will be a soloist with the Boston Symphony Orchestra this season is shown at right with her "Peke." (Savona)

DR. SERGE KOUSSEVITZKY, conductor of the Boston Symphony Orchestra, in a picture made while climbing in the Swiss Alps. This year he spent his vacation in America for the first time, climbing mountains in New Hampshire.

JASCHA HEIFETZ, eminent violinist, makes many of his own arrangements, a task which kept him occupied during the vacation period.

GREGOR PIATIGORSKY, 'cellist, polishing up his cello in preparation for a busy concert season.

SERGEI RACHMANINOFF, the celebrated pianist is shown here in his New York Home—(left). At the left, OLGA AVERINO, Boston soprano, is the daughter of Nicholas Avierino, viola player in the Boston Symphony Orchestra, and the wife of Paul Federovsky, one of the first violinists in Dr. Koussevitzky's organization.

PAUL ALTHOUSE, leading American tenor at the left and SERGE PROKOFIEFF, composer-pianist, who will play his own Third Concerto with the Boston Symphony Orchestra during the coming season.

Keith Lockhart
The Next Generation

Keith Lockhart is the conductor of the Boston Symphony Youth Concerts, which reach more than 40,000 children and families each season.

There are two different ways to approach Family and Outreach concerts; I believe both are valid. The first is to take the orchestra to the people, to their own turf: to perform in church basements, multi-purpose rooms, and school auditoriums—venues in which people are comfortable and open to new experiences, even if these spaces may not present the orchestra to best advantage. The other approach is to welcome people to the orchestra's home, Symphony Hall—a building that not only presents the orchestra at its best but also engenders a significantly different experience than can a school cafeteria. Bringing people into the hall instills in new audiences—even kids who have no real background or previous exposure—the sense of awe that all of us feel about live symphonic music. There is something about this place that sets just the right stage for music-making. A live performance is an extraordinary event to be a part of, and this hall was built for extraordinary events. And the hall is really an instrument—like a violin but much bigger and a little less portable! It is the instrument that the orchestra "plays," and it's integral to the sound and experience. You see kids who have been squirming like mad on their way in, but when they sit down in this special place and the music starts, everything changes. They're rapt, focused. And that is a great experience to have early in life.

I didn't have a lot of great musical experiences as a youngster because I didn't have concert-going parents. One of the first things I remember is going to New York, to the Met, when I was in third or fourth grade (it was called the "New Met" then). We were there to see a dress rehearsal open to students. The thing is, I remember very little about that performance; I don't think I was particularly attuned. But I do remember the feeling of being in the space—I remember thinking that whatever was going to go on in that space must be incredible. It must be very, very important. I went back to my elementary school much changed by the experience.

Above, children in front of Symphony Hall; below, children enjoying a Boston Symphony Youth Concert with Keith Lockhart

Harry Ellis Dickson
Memories of Youth

In 1949 Boston Symphony violinist Harry Ellis Dickson established the Boston Symphony Orchestra Youth Concerts. Dickson persuaded local philanthropists to underwrite the concerts, and he coordinated the scheduling of Boston Symphony Orchestra members, who had to be engaged unofficially. In addition, Dickson recruited volunteers to spread the word because he strongly believed that the city needed a permanent youth concert program to reach out to young people and their families. In his book, Beating Time, *Dickson proudly notes that "Youth Concerts at Symphony Hall" have now become "The Boston Symphony Youth Concerts" and are part of the Orchestra's regular schedule, and, since they started, more than a million children and families have attended the concerts in Symphony Hall.*

In his book, Dickson conveys his philosophy and talks about the early years of the youth concerts:

When the series started, Isaac Stern, who was appearing with the Boston Symphony that week (in a subscription concert), agreed to be the soloist at the first concert, on a Saturday morning. I remember how quietly interested the youngsters were, not only in his playing, but in his down-to-earth remarks and explanations. He asked how many play the violin and, after getting a show of hands, said, "It's tough to play the violin, isn't it? You probably get discouraged as I did. But you must stick with it." He went on to explain how musicians must train their hearing, their muscular coordination, and so on. Stern played a G-major scale, slightly out of tune, and with a rather unpleasant, steely sound. "That's the way we all sound when we begin," he said. "But with practice you develop your ear and control, and you begin to sound better." He played the scale again, this time beautifully, and the audience burst into applause. We then played the finale of the Mendelssohn Concerto, first illustrating the themes and showing that the composer sometimes allows the orchestra to play the melody while the soloist accompanies it and vice versa, then the entire movement without pause. This humanistic approach to music, so charmingly carried out by Stern, is what we have been striving for in our youth concerts ever since.

The programs were varied, and we played music from the pre-Baroque period to the ultra-modern, including an occasional avant-garde piece, which is much easier for a young person, without adult prejudices to accept, than it is for his or her parents. We have even presented programs of jazz and music based on jazz, never attempting to influence the listeners, but presenting all the aspects of music and letting them make up their own minds.

Especially interesting to me was our experiment with music other than the loud and bombastic. Each program contained at least one short, quiet piece when the audience was invited to listen in silent contemplation. One of the more successful compositions was a work by the American composer Michael Colgrass, *As Quiet As...* Before playing it we announced that we were about to test the fine acoustics of Symphony Hall, and in the ensuing stillness we dropped a pin on the stage, inviting those in the second balcony to listen for it. "Yes!" they cried.

If we have learned anything about young people, it was that we must never play down to them. I am firmly convinced that children's interests are not limited to special music for the young. They can listen to all kinds, including some too "deep" for their elders. The only compromise one need make is to their attention span.

The Boston Symphony Youth Concerts, now under the leadership of Keith Lockhart, continue to evolve and inspire a new generation of children. Over the years the Orchestra has expanded its youth outreach beyond the annual concert series to a mentoring program in the Boston schools, a community concert series geared toward families, a resource center for teachers, and a commitment to advocating for music education in public schools. In the new millennium the Boston Symphony Orchestra has renewed its commitment to build on the legacy of Harry Ellis Dickson by increasing the scope of BSO youth and educational activities.

A young boy checking on tickets at the box office

CONDUCTOR SERGE KOUSSEVITZKY pauses to smile his approval of the morning's work. His right hand clutches the handkerchief with which he has been mopping his face. He wears the longish jacket with button cuffs which is his rehearsal "uniform." Over his shoulders is thrown the black cloak which he dons the instant he stops work.

RICHARD BURGIN
Concertmaster

FERNAND GILLET
First Oboe

GLOBE STAFF PHOTOS
ARTHUR GRIFFIN

JACOB RAICHMAN
First Trombone

WILLEM VALKENIER
First Horn

BERNARD ZIGHERA
First Harp

LOUIS SPEYER
English Horn

VICTOR POLATSCHEK
First Clarinet

GEORGES LAURENT
First Flute

JEAN BEDETTI
First Cello

JEAN LEFRANC
First Viola

ROMAN SZULC
Tympani

GEORGES MOLEUX
First Bass

LUKAS FOSS
Piano

GEORGES MAGER
First Trumpet

Symphony Aces at Rehearsal

By CYRUS DURGIN, Globe Music Critic

HOURS OF EXHAUSTING REHEARSAL precede the magnificent concerts of the Boston Symphony Orchestra. Every morning Monday through Thursday at Symphony Hall Serge Koussevitzky works with the virtuosi he has fashioned into what has been called "the greatest orchestra in the world." Now in his 22d year as conductor, Koussevitzky is a merciless taskmaster and spares neither himself nor his men in the preparation of his vivid interpretations. The Globe's Arthur Griffin took his camera to a rehearsal the other morning and came away with some views of the conductor and the leaders of the various sections of the orchestra, called in musical jargon, "first desk men." This is how they look as they play.

Koussevitzky and the orchestra maintained an important relationship with the composer Igor Stravinsky. Like Koussevitzky, Stravinsky was Russian but worked in France until the first rumblings of World War II, when he moved to the United States—to Boston, then Hollywood. Among the important premieres of Stravinsky's work were the Concerto for Piano and Winds, in 1925, *Oedipus Rex*, in 1928, the Violin Concerto, in 1932, and *Four Norwegian Moods* and *Orpheus*, in the 1940s.

The orchestra began specifically to commission new music, a dozen works invited from as many composers, for its fiftieth anniversary in 1930-1931. An astonishing number of the resulting works have been recognized as among the masterpieces of the century—in particular, Stravinsky's *Symphony of Psalms*, as well as Hindemith's Concert Music for Strings and Brass, Howard Hanson's Second Symphony, Prokofiev's Fourth, Roussel's Third, and Copland's *Symphonic Ode*. The Symphony's practice of commissioning a body of new work has continued for all major anniversaries and has spread to virtually all professional orchestras in the United States.

Not the least of Koussevitzky's contributions to the musical resonance of Symphony Hall—and to American musical life—was his determination to introduce the pieces he most admired, even in the face of audience puzzlement, by offering them again and again until the average concertgoer was comfortable. *Symphony of Psalms*, which, at its premiere in December 1930, met incomprehension and passionate debate about whether such music could be "religious," was simply brought back. He programmed it again the following February, then repeated it the next season (April 1932), and then every three to five years (April 1936, April 1939, April 1942, and March 1947) until his retirement.

Music Director Serge Koussevitzky and the principal players are featured in this special Boston Globe *pictorial section, October 21, 1945.*

Steven Spielberg
Rolling

John Williams, Steven Spielberg, and Itzhak Perlman in Symphony Hall while recording the soundtrack of Schindler's List, *1993*

Since I'm not a Bostonian and not a musician—although I would count myself as a music-lover—I came to know Symphony Hall through my dear friend and colleague, John Williams. When Johnny was appointed as conductor of the Boston Pops two decades ago, it wasn't long before he was saying to me, "You've got to come to Boston and see this place." Since then, I've had absolutely wonderful experiences here, both as an audience member and as part of my professional life. We had the singular honor of recording both *Schindler's List* and *Saving Private Ryan* in Symphony Hall with the magnificent Boston Symphony Orchestra. The first one was *Schindler's*, and it has to have been one of the most emotional moments of my life—the night Itzhak Perlman first played

through John's score with the Boston Symphony. Then, several years later, I'll never forget sitting in the first balcony with Tom Hanks amid such elegance and splendor and hearing that orchestra play John's "Hymn to the Fallen" from *Private Ryan*.

I think today that Symphony Hall is an instrument. Acoustically, it's a member of the orchestra. I found that it lent itself to creating a very emotional, rich sound that I wanted to infuse in both of my films. In special instances, music is the most important part of a film. I know my films would not have enjoyed half the success they have over the years if it weren't for John Williams's talent and genius. And to that, I now acknowledge the genius and beauty of Symphony Hall.

John Williams

Symphony Hall in the Dark

The surest way to commune with the spirit of Symphony Hall is to sit in it, late at night, alone in the near dark, when it's lit by a single worklight on the stage. This is a unique experience, available only to a privileged few, but it is one that I've relished many times—and is one that I'm happy to speak about.

Quite often after concerts, while waiting to go home, I wander into the hall to stop and ponder and, most of all, to listen. The time is typically about an hour or so after the end of a concert, not long after the hall was filled with people—all playing, singing, listening, and applauding, and sometimes even standing and cheering in the balconies.

I sense that I can still hear echoes of what transpired in the hall earlier that evening, and the sound is not faint—it's actually quite loud! It's as though the hall has a memory bank that stores in the molecules of its walls all of the sounds it creates with the orchestra and the audience.

Both the immediate and distant past seem to live in this place. I wonder what the walls might "remember" of Koussevitzky or Prokofiev, or what they might tell us about Tchaikovsky's visit or Rachmaninoff's sound. All of these wonders seem to be mysteriously and magically stored here. I like to think that the seats, walls, and floors of the hall are all distant cousins of the wood vibrating in our violins, violas, and basses, and that they all conjoin to make each concert a kind of "celebration of the trees,"

whose spirit carries the message of the music to us. In this way, the hall functions as an equal partner with the instruments themselves, performing its wonders again and again as it tirelessly aids us in our quest to "apprehend the transcendent."

The Story of My Grandfather's Hammer

My French-speaking maternal grandfather, David Towner, stood six-feet-three. He was powerfully built, and might have been regarded as an impressive figure by his generation of peers. He was a carpenter and cabinet-maker by trade, who emigrated from the province of Quebec to the city of Boston in 1890. There, he married and raised a family of ten children, the youngest being my mother, who was born in 1909.

Throughout my childhood in the 1930s, while my grandfather was still alive, I spent summers at my grandmother's house in Natick. There, we children were told over and over again the story of grandfather David's hammer. It seems that during the 1890s and beyond, he worked on many public buildings in Boston, including Symphony Hall and Horticultural Hall. He also contributed cabinets for the Museum of Fine Arts. Grandfather David always worked with his personal tools, which he marked by carving his initials.

One day, while working high on an uncompleted wall at Symphony Hall, he inadvertently dropped his hammer into the space between the inner and outer walls. It fell many feet into the darkness below, becoming lost to my grandfather forever.

Judging by the number of times he told the story, I think my grandfather took consolation in the fact that he'd left something of such a personal nature deep within this special building. In the same way, I find joy in the knowledge that somewhere within these walls lies a hammer with the initials "D.T." on it, claimed by the hall itself, where it remains to this day and beyond—a silent but proud remembrance of one of the many strong hands that built this place.

John Williams, Boston Pops laureate conductor,
in the first balcony of Symphony Hall, spring 2000

Small wonder, then, that Symphony Hall was considered the hub of contemporary music in those years. Even so, to talk about only the new would overlook Koussevitzky's renown as a conductor of the nineteenth-century masters, from Beethoven to Tchaikovsky, and his devotion to the great choral works of Bach, which he performed with fervor and devotion, and to Beethoven's *Missa Solemnis*, which he led in its second Boston performance in 1927.

The task of succeeding Koussevitzky fell to Charles Munch (1891-1968), who combined in his culture and training both the French and German elements that were so important to the repertory and the audience; still, his genial manner could hardly have been more different from Koussevitzky's passionate intensity. Munch supervised the orchestra's commissioning program for its seventy-fifth anniversary, which resulted in Roger Sessions's Third Symphony, William Schuman's

Top to bottom, Charles Munch (1891-1968), music director from 1949 to 1962; Erich Leinsdorf, Charles Munch, and Pierre Monteux, c. 1963; William Steinberg (1899-1978), music director, 1969-1972

Seventh, Martinů's Sixth, Leonard Bernstein's Third, and Henri Dutilleux's Second (*Le Double*), among others. Other Americans whose works were premiered during Munch's tenure were Schuman (Violin Concerto, Seventh Symphony), David Diamond (Third Symphony), Nicolas Nabakov (*La vita nuova*), Irving Fine (Symphony), Lukas Foss (Piano Concerto No. 2), Alexei Haieff (Concerto for Piano; Symphony No. 2), and Walter Piston (Viola Concerto). Munch also introduced a considerable amount of French music, including Poulenc's Piano Concerto and *Gloria*, Milhaud's Fourth Piano Concerto and *Suite concertante*, Honegger's Symphony No. 5, Jean Martinon's *Hymne à la vie* and Prelude and Toccata, Florent Schmitt's Symphony No. 2, and Jacques Ibert's *Bostoniana*.

For all his charm and popularity, Munch was never an exacting taskmaster in the manner of Gericke or Monteux. Erich Leinsdorf (1912-1993) reasserted the great German traditions of the past and tightened up the orchestra's playing. Just as significantly, he programmed imaginative combinations of works (many of them new to the BSO repertory), initiated the performance of complete operas in concert form with the BSO, founded the Boston Symphony Chamber Players, and led the orchestra in numerous important premieres, including works by Benjamin Britten, Elliott Carter, Benjamin Lees, Walter Piston, Gunther Schuller, and Roger Sessions.

Leinsdorf's short tenure was followed by the even shorter one (owing to illness) of William Steinberg (1899-1978). During that period, Michael Tilson Thomas, serving initially as assistant conductor (1969-1970), then associate conductor, and finally as the first principal guest conductor (with Colin Davis) from 1972 to 1974, then led the last of many Boston premieres of Walter Piston (Flute Concerto), as well as William Schuman (*Concerto on Old English Rounds*), Oliver Knussen (Third Symphony), and Edison Denisov (Concerto for flute, oboe, piano, and orchestra). At the same time, Colin Davis, as principal guest conductor from 1972 through 1984, began introducing Boston, and the country, to the work of Sir Michael Tippett.

Seiji Ozawa, whose music directorship has surpassed Koussevitzky's in longevity, succeeded Steinberg in 1973. Ozawa's brilliant technique in even the most difficult music, whether the large symphonies of Gustav Mahler or an abstruse modern score, forged a new virtuosity in the orchestra and made it possible to bring in much new repertoire. Ozawa introduced works by leading Japanese composers, notably Toru Takemitsu, and continued Munch's close connection with French music, especially that of Olivier Messiaen and, in later years, Henri Dutilleux. With the appointment of the Dutch conductor Bernard Haitink as principal guest conductor in 1995, Boston Symphony audiences have been offered an interpretive perspective that is connected in many ways to the orchestra's Germanic early years.

The single largest series of new works performed during Ozawa's tenure was the dozen commissions for the Symphony's centennial, in 1981. They included four works by Boston composers (John Harbison, Donald Martino, Peter Lieberson, and Leon Kirchner), four by other American composers (Leonard Bernstein, Roger Sessions, Olly Wilson, and John Corigliano), and four by Europeans (Peter Maxwell Davies, Sir Michael Tippett, Sándor Balassa, and Andrzej Panufnik). Other new music (including many noncommissions as well as commissions not connected to anniversaries) included works by John Cage, Bernard Rands, Stephen Albert, Christopher Rouse, Hans Werner Henze, Sofia Gubaidulina, and George Walker. Ozawa also began to offer concert stagings of complete operas at Symphony Hall and at Tanglewood, with a platform built above the orchestra for the movement of the singers. In this way, Boston Symphony audiences

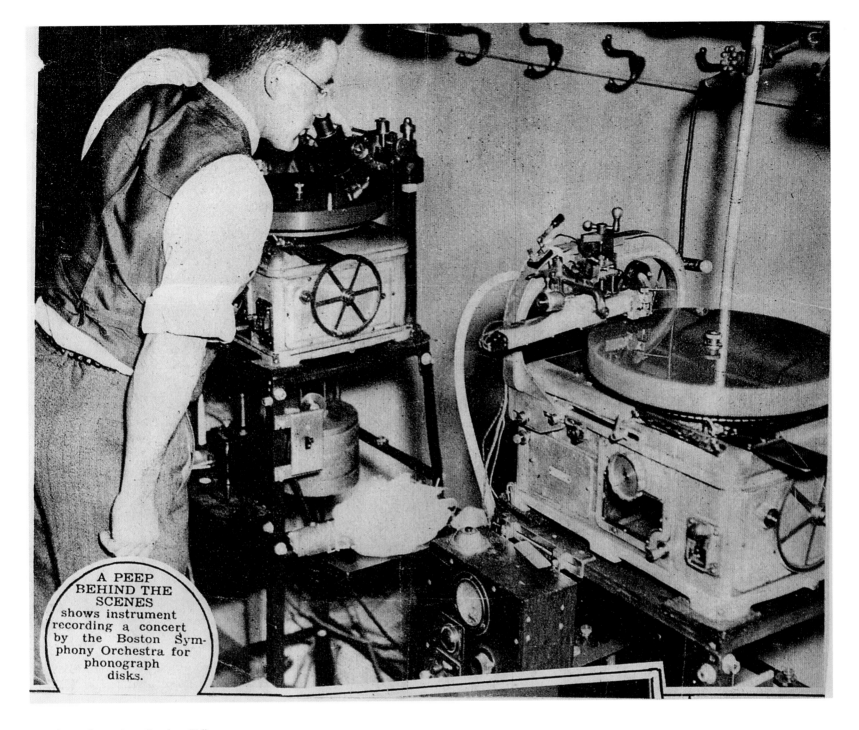

A PEEP BEHIND THE SCENES shows instrument recording a concert by the Boston Symphony Orchestra for phonograph disks.

An early recording session at Symphony Hall,
c. 1935

heard Gluck's *Orfeo*, Berg's *Wozzeck*, Strauss's *Salome* and *Elektra*, Verdi's *Falstaff*, Tchaikovsky's *Queen of Spades*, Stravinsky's *Rake's Progress*, and Puccini's *Madama Butterfly*.

And always, along with the commissions, the novelties, and the rarities, Symphony Hall has resounded through the years with the enormous repertory for orchestra that encompasses the musical creativity of an increasingly large number of the world's nationalities and races.

OUTSIDE EVENTS

The principal purpose of Symphony Hall is to provide a home for the Boston Symphony and the Boston Pops orchestras. Even at full throttle, however, the orchestra does not give concerts every night. Of the many other organizations that appear regularly in the hall, the most venerable is the Handel & Haydn Society, whose founding goes back more than sixty-five years before that of the Symphony. In the early years, the group was a self-governing organization of amateur singers. Later,

RECORDING THE EXTRAORDINARY SOUND

Through its prolific recording, the Boston Symphony Orchestra has brought the incredible sound of both the BSO and Symphony Hall to audiences worldwide. The first record was made in 1917, under the leadership of Karl Muck. Each recording demonstrates the interests and artistic direction of its music director as well as the sound of the orchestra at a particular time. And the cover art for the albums and CDs shows the changing aesthetic trends in classical music promotion.

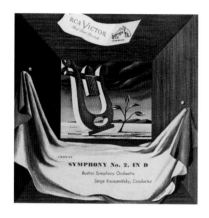

1935

1944

1945

1946

1946

1946

1947

1955

1955

1956

1957

1958

1958

1959

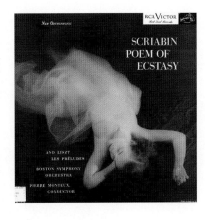

1959

1961

1968

1968

1972

1976

1979

1980

1981

1999

the choice of repertory broadened, but, for the most part, it consisted of the major baroque and classical oratorios. In the last third of the twentieth century, the Society became fully professional (and much smaller in size), first under Thomas Dunn, then Christopher Hogwood, and, since the fall of 2000, Grant Llewellyn.

The Celebrity Series—now called the FleetBoston Celebrity Series, and originally called the Aaron Richmond Concerts—has brought distinguished recitalists, chamber ensembles, and touring orchestras to Symphony Hall for more than sixty years. Sunday afternoons and Friday evenings frequently find an audience for a favorite singer, string quartet, or piano soloist, or perhaps a visit-

Erich Leinsdorf talking with Seiji Ozawa in 1979; at right, Ozawa conducting the BSO during the 1999-2000 season

Seiji Ozawa

First Impressions

What is the expression in English—you can't judge a book by its cover? I tell you why I say this: The first time I conducted in Symphony Hall was in 1968. I had already conducted at Tanglewood, but this was my first invitation to Boston. My wife and I came from Toronto, where I was music director, and we had to bring our dog, a Yorkshire terrier. The only hotel that would take us was what is now the Eliot, at the corner of Massachusetts and Commonwealth avenues. It was pretty bad then. At least I could walk to the hall, I was told.

The first morning I had a shock. I started to walk, and I saw some very strange, very dirty shops; bad Chinese restaurants even I wouldn't go in, strange people too. When I got closer to this big brick building at the end of Mass. Ave., I decided it couldn't be Symphony Hall. You know, I had some fantasy about it: Symphony Hall must look very fancy, with a nice sign, but I saw nothing. So I asked, and found out, yes, this was it. I walked in and went upstairs. I remember there was a big welcome, and I felt very happy.

The next thing I remember is standing on that amazing stage. The hall looked so beautiful to me. I could feel so much dignity and tradition. But nothing prepared me for the sound of the Boston Symphony—so warm, and clear, and effortless. I am convinced that what we know as the "Boston Symphony sound" has been created by these acoustics. The orchestra never has to force or push. The sound just flies.

I fell in love then, and have been ever since. It's true. I think about what genius it was, at the beginning of that new century, to have made this hall. How brave it was, too. I wonder what it was like to see it being built. How huge it must have looked, and what a risk it must have seemed like. Would it work? Would it sound right? Would it be full? Who could imagine how lucky I would be, how lucky all of us are, to live in such a place?

From a press conference, April 2000

ing orchestra from elsewhere in the United States, Europe, or Asia. Even before the founding of the Celebrity Series, there has been a long tradition of recitals in Symphony Hall. Among the great artists who performed were the pianists Sergei Rachmaninoff, Claudio Arrau, Rudolf Serkin, Harold Bauer, Josef Hofmann, Vladimir Horowitz, Ignace Paderewski, and Arthur Rubinstein. Violinists included Mischa Elman, Fritz Kreisler, Jascha Heifetz, Yehudi Menuhin, and Isaac Stern. Singers included John McCormack, Feodor Chaliapin, Geraldine Farrar, Amelita Galli-Curci, Louise Homer, Lawrence Tibbett, Marian Anderson, and Jessye Norman. Some of them benefited from the 1917 concert in which the young African-American tenor Roland Hayes rented Symphony Hall himself for a recital of German *Lieder* and other classical repertory; its success assured that the hall would be open to musicians of all races.

TODAY AND THE FUTURE

More than ever, Symphony Hall is a monument to music for all Bostonians, all visitors to Boston, and all who hear recordings or broadcasts that originated in the hall. From schoolchildren who attend the youth concerts to subscribers who have been attending concerts for sixty years or more, from the family attending a Pops concert to the visitor enjoying a favorite artist in recital, Symphony Hall stands—as it has stood for an entire century—at the very center of Boston's musical life.

Beethoven still presides. His music resounds against the wood and plaster of the walls, echoes into the deepest crevices of the ornate ceiling, bounces around and behind the statues in their niches and into the ears of some 2,500 listeners when the auditorium is full. It is not only Beethoven's music that resounds, of course, but that of his many and extremely diverse successors, to say nothing of the older masters from whom he learned his art. These walls have absorbed a century of sound, and they stand ready to absorb and reflect the energy of the coming century as well. If Beethoven could have imagined the myriad effects that his own music, and his example as a symbol of human creativity, was destined to have in faraway America, he would no doubt have been greatly astonished. But he would have been proud as well. ✍

—*Steven Ledbetter*

CONSTANTINE MANOS

PORTRAIT OF A SYMPHONY
1960 & 2000

From the introduction to
Portrait of a Symphony, *1960*

Have you ever been a lone listener in the presence of a live symphony orchestra? Have you ever had the experience of hearing a hundred men perform for yourself alone? I boast of having been that lucky: Composers who wait patiently to hear their own work rehearsed may occasionally find the auditorium emptied of all listeners but themselves. Without their being aware of it, more than one orchestra has played for me alone. Each such experience remains in my mind as a rare treat.

An equivalent treat awaits the viewer who turns the pages of this book of photographs. Here too, it seems to me, one may enjoy the vicarious pleasure of finding oneself, like the composer, alone in the presence of a great orchestra.

Think for a moment what a full-fledged orchestra is. This disparate conglomeration of personalities and talents is truly an entity like a nation; it is a living thing that breathes and moves in ways peculiar to its own being. At its head is a leader who, through bodily gestures and facial expressivity, acts out the music's progress. There are subtle understandings between leader and instrumentalists, psychological adjustments between player and player, or section and section, all intent on achieving a single goal—the illumination of the composer's thought.

An orchestra is fully aware of its own power. It knows it can be awe-inspiring and nerve shattering, enraged and inconsolable, and then as suddenly melt us with a dulcet and almost feminine grace.

To the real *aficionado*, any aspect of an orchestra's activity is of interest. The backstage preparations, the drama of the tuning room, the gossip of the corridors, the gathering of the audience out front—these are the mundane scenes that balance and accompany the more brilliant action. Everyone from the ticket-taker to the man who encases the harp for the night is charged with the glamour of an orchestra.

Of all our symphony orchestras, the one that has the most glamour for me is the one that makes its home in Symphony Hall. For thirty-five years I have seen the musical development of our age mirrored in their playing. I count myself among the many thousands of their admirers who will have much joy from possessing these visual impressions of this great orchestra. ✑

—*Aaron Copland*

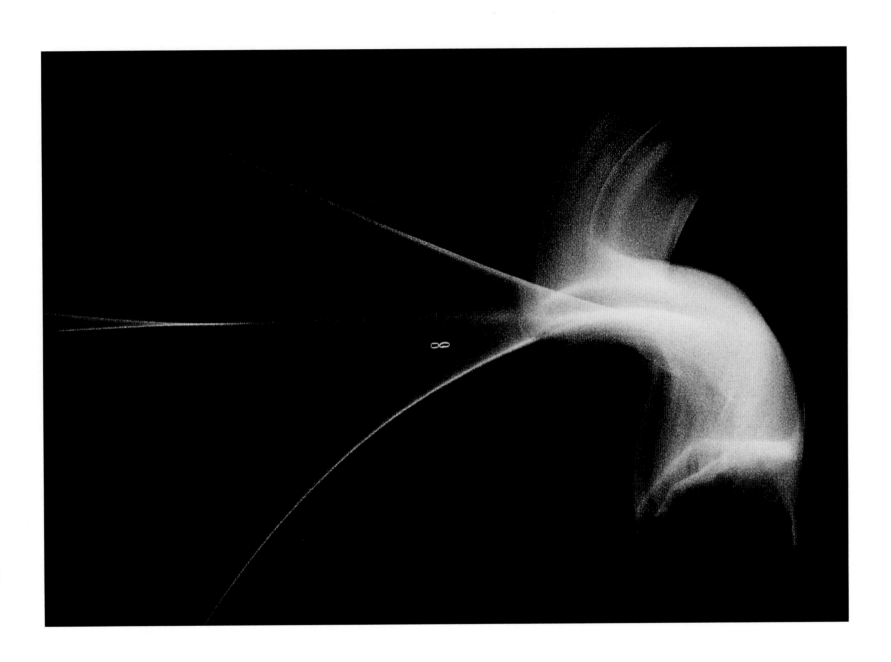

The Boston Pops:
From Promenade
to Esplanade

The Boston Pops in Symphony Hall

Henry Lee Higginson had yet another vision for his beloved city of Boston:

To give in Boston as many serious concerts of classical music as were wanted and also to give at other times, and more especially in the summer, concerts of a lighter kind of music, in which should be included good dance music....

The result, as we know today, was the Boston Pops. The first of these light classical performances—originally known as "Promenade Concerts"—started in the summer of 1885 in the Boston Music Hall. As Higginson wished, they included dance music and were modeled after European light classical concerts: the Proms in London and the ambiance of an outdoor German beer garden. The programs were immediately popular; one Boston newspaper described them as so well attended and enjoyed that a newcomer might assume they had been produced for years. The Boston *Journal*'s music critic wrote a review in 1895 describing the audience response to the concerts:

There was honest enjoyment, thanks to conductor and orchestra. There was no trying to like a thing, because somebody had previously said it was great, or because it was stamped with the portentous seal of some eminent, deep-chested and long-haired Leipziger Professor or some Berlin Music Doctor. There was rhythm in plenty, and there were tunes that set feet in motion and eyes to sparkling.

That same year, a *Globe* reporter wrote, "...the audience responded so heartily that the encores and extras were doubling the length of the program," while the *Boston Transcript* added, "Those who wished to concentrate on the music evidently found that they could hear all they wanted, judging from the frequent applause and calls for repetitions."

At right, Vauxhall Gardens in London, one of the European "pleasure gardens," charged a small fee for admission and offered music and refreshments; below, Vienna's Volksgarten, a popular beer and wine garden, featured music, dancing, and refreshments.

The social aspect of these concerts was unique to the city at the time. With two intermissions, there was considerable opportunity for socializing and "promenading." Thus, Pops became an integral part of the city's summer social scene, with reviews frequently including descriptions of the ladies' fashions. One newspaper reported, "Pretty gowns of light fabrics made a flutter of many colors. It was too Bohemian a place for regulation evening gowns. In their place were many daring combinations, a little risqué for a parlor, but 'quite the thing' for 'pop.'"

Sixteen years after the Pops concerts were founded, Symphony Hall was built as the venue for both the Boston Symphony and Boston Pops. To accommodate the very different performance forms, the architects designed the auditorium with a configuration featuring banked rows of seating for the winter season of Symphony concerts and a flat floor for the Pops season. The latter provided for cabaret seating, with chairs ringed around tables. To this day, this conversion is accomplished by an ingenious system of risers that can be removed or replaced in a couple of days—moving in and out of the basement of Symphony Hall through a large elevator, hidden in the middle of the auditorium. One unique aspect of the hall is that it is acoustically superior for both traditional classical concerts and the more lively Pops. While many halls have been retrofitted to duplicate the Boston Pops ambiance—with tables and chairs—Symphony Hall was the first specifically planned for dual formats.

In 1901, when the Pops concerts moved into the new hall, the concerts were officially named Pops—shortened from "popular" concerts. With the move to this hall and its great sound, management hoped that socializing would become secondary to the enjoyment and appreciation of the music. There was some concern that, in the past, newspapers had concentrated on the socialites in attendance rather than the music. In an effort to make the evening more musically relevant to both patrons and reviewers, the program noted that during certain pieces the audience was requested to "preserve silence during the performance." On opening night, the *Boston Globe* reviewer commented on the music and the ambiance and included a complete list of the evening's program. With the headline "First of the 'Pop' concerts," the review began, "It was all perfectly natural. There was the same dignified and picturesque audience, the same cultivated 'sang froid,' the same beautiful music (only more so) and the same old feeling of kinship and fellowship among the 2000 or more people who attended the opening of the 'Pops' at Symphony Hall last evening."

An enthusiastic Herald *review after the opening "pop" concert at Symphony Hall*

THE BOSTON HERALD — TUESDAY, MAY 6, 1902.

"POP" CONCERT SEASON OPENS WITH A BIG CROWD AND ENCORES AND DOUBLE ENCORES

OPENING NIGHT OF THE "POPS" AT SYMPHONY HALL.

Even in the new hall, the heritage of the German beer gardens remained. For many years, the hall was decorated to replicate the feeling of outdoor space; the walls were painted dark green each season, while shrubbery and plants were placed throughout the floor. Smoking was so prevalent that, on many evenings, smoke shrouded the balconies by the latter part of the evening.

While management may have been successful in promoting music over socializing on many Pops evenings, it certainly did not on "college nights." These special concerts, which continue to this day, were held for graduating seniors and their guests (women were seated in the balconies

METAMORPHOSIS

Each spring and each December, Symphony Hall's auditorium is transformed. The leather-covered seats (about 1492 in all), and even the slanting floor on the orchestra level of the hall, are removed and stored in a far wing of the basement. 288 oddly shaped tables, each assigned five green-and-gold folding chairs, replace the black rows of Symphony seats. And the hall is ready for Pops!

Each time this transformation takes place, the Boston Symphony hires twenty-five extra laborers, men and women, who are supervised by the BSO's year-round crew. The changeover takes about eight hours. As three groups of laborers remove the first rows of seats, two workers on mechanics' creepers inch their way under the slanted portion of the floor at the rear of the hall, unbolting the steel framework that supports those seats.

By the time the crews finish the front half of the hall, the rear half is ready for dismantling. To facilitate storage and the retransformation of the auditorium for the BSO season, the laborers store the rows of seats, sections of floor, and steel frame in a very specific order.

These components are loaded on carts, lowered through the floor on an elevator near the center of the hall and manually wheeled down the long cement ramp under the Cohen Wing. A forklift operator jockeys each stack of seats into its proper storage position.

The floor removal process requires 160 trips on the elevator, a two-ton hydraulic piston unit installed in 1987. The original elevator was water-operated.

only). The first college nights included MIT, Harvard, and Tufts. One story recounts how on Harvard Night in 1901—called "the rowdiest evening in the history of concerts"—"the students screamed and shouted, sang their college songs while the orchestra played programmed music, and rearranged the furniture to perform interesting acrobatic feats." Some say that only with the start of Prohibition were they really able to focus the audience on the music.

During the early years of Pops, there was no appointed conductor; two or three members of the orchestra shared this duty. The first regular conductor was Agide Jacchia, a fiery Italian who led the Pops through most of the Prohibition era; even without alcohol, the concerts were popular and well-attended thanks to his appeal. After Jacchia's departure at the end of the 1926 season, a young Boston Symphony Orchestra violinist named Arthur Fiedler sought the position, but he was rejected in favor of the European composer, pianist, and conductor Alfredo Casella. During that time, Fiedler was becoming known in Boston by establishing a series of increasingly well-attended concerts on the Esplanade along the Charles River, played with his own pickup orchestra. After Casella's brief and unsuccessful tenure, Fiedler was selected as the next conductor.

Arthur Fiedler conducting the Pops in the 1950s; below, Fiedler, c. 1930

When Fiedler took over the Pops in 1930, he was the first American to hold the position; he quickly made his mark by ensuring that American popular music was included in the programs. Fiedler believed that the Pops should be lively and keep up with current musical trends. He discussed his programming philosophy in one interview:

It struck me that this general public was snobbish about what they called "classical" music, and the "classical-minded" crowd was snobbish about music which they called "popular" with an air of condescension. Accordingly, I laid out programs in three sections so planned to provide something of interest for the greatest variety of tastes in the course of the evening. In this way, various hostile camps listened to music which they thought they did not like or understand, but which in reality they had not listened to. They discovered that "popular" music is familiar music.

Fiedler's legacy of a tripartite program continues today. So too do his traditions of taking the Boston Pops to the national stage through prolific recordings and the *Evening at Pops* television program.

A history of the Boston Pops must include Harry Ellis Dickson, who still conducts the orchestra in the year 2000, after forty-five years of Boston Pops conducting accolades. Fiedler developed a close relationship with Dickson when the latter was a member of the first violin section of the orchestra. In the 1955 season, Fiedler asked Dickson to step in for him as conductor while he recuperated from an operation—thereby missing almost the entire season. Subsequently, Fiedler appointed Dickson assistant conductor, both out of respect for his musical ability and because of the trust between them.

Dickson is noted for the humorous anecdotes he tells about Arthur Fiedler and the musicians. One such story recounts the "running battle over his [Dickson's] practice of stealing batons from Arthur Fiedler's drawer." The battle culminated after Fiedler's last concert at Symphony Hall, when he summoned Dickson to his room to ask "Did you swipe my baton?" as he was being treated by paramedics before going to the hospital. Dickson, who now holds the position of associate laureate conductor, is known as the elder statesman of the Boston Pops and is well respected for his work through the years at Symphony Hall, on tour with the Boston Pops, and on *Evening at Pops*.

Keith Lockhart

"America's Orchestra"

This is a country that is extraordinarily diverse, incredibly spread out, and fiercely independent at all levels: town, state, country. If you look at a country like Austria, for instance, it has a "national" opera and a "national" orchestra, the Vienna State Opera and the Vienna Philharmonic. Elsewhere in Europe there is the Paris Opera, one of the national art institutions of France; in England, the London Symphony is arguably the flagship orchestra of the country. It is hard to find a parallel situation in the United States. (No New Yorker would agree that the Boston Symphony is the country's preeminent orchestral institution, for instance... or vice versa, for that matter.) There is no orchestra that is popularly pointed to and embraced by everybody across the country as "national"—except the Boston Pops. This is because the Boston Pops is unique: It provides a different menu of music in a different way than any other large orchestra—and it transcends boundaries.

From the beginning, the Boston Pops has been outreach-driven—even before people used the term. Indefatigable touring started fifty years ago, and the orchestra has a recording legacy second to none. By the time most households owned a Victrola, almost every one of them had an Arthur Fiedler/Boston Pops 78 sitting on top of it. Tours and recordings moved the orchestra from Symphony Hall and Boston to the nation. Television increased the impact and reach of the orchestra still further. For over thirty years, the Boston Pops has been broadcast into homes of every shape and size and viewed by families, not only in large urban areas, but also in areas that have no significant cultural institutions. But touring, recording, and television wouldn't have bestowed the title "America's Orchestra" on the Boston Pops if the music hadn't been universally appealing—whether people grew up on big band, country, rock, pop, or classical music. There is a true affection for the orchestra throughout the country.

The easiest way to witness this affection is to leave Symphony Hall and Boston and observe the reactions you get when the orchestra performs in

Keith Lockhart applauding the orchestra in 1999

Idaho. People talk about their drive from Oklahoma to see the concert, worth the effort because they always wanted to hear the Boston Pops live after watching *Evening at Pops* for so many years, after listening to the records and CDs. There is no other arts organization that they would do this for. And this special fondness

and enthusiasm—as if you are the home team even when playing on an away court—is unique in this country. And it is immensely gratifying to be part of an organization that can have such an impact on people's lives.

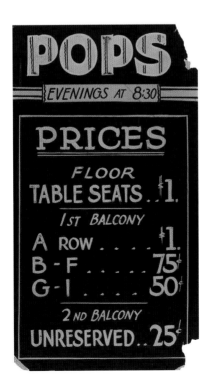

Pops posters from the 1930s and 1940s

ON RECORD: REFLECTIONS OF CHANGING TIMES

The Boston Pops has recorded hundreds of albums, many of which have risen to the top of the charts. Arthur Fiedler, in particular, made a significant number of records. Each one reflects current trends in popular music; the cover art, in itself, shows how styles of art direction, illustration, and photography have changed over the years.

1946

1950

1950

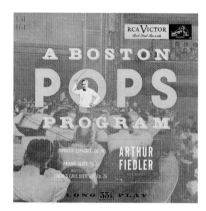

1951

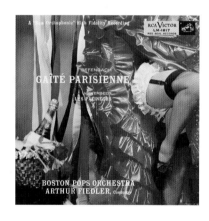

1954

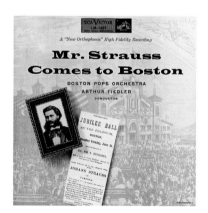

1955

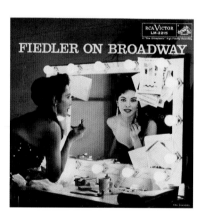

1958

1958

1959

1959

1959

1960

1961

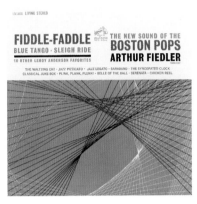

1962

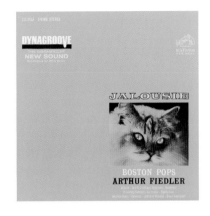

1963

1968

1969

1972

1973

1979

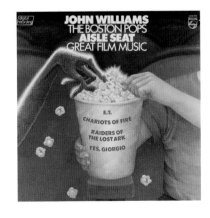

1982

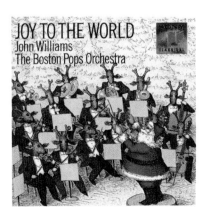

1991

1996

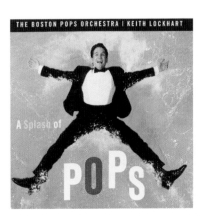

1999

Opus 1

The piano recital. Ah yes, for those who took piano lessons at the age of eight or whatever, the recital was surely the most traumatic event of young lives—to sit down, stiff-fingered, in a strange living room, one's parents standing in the back looking woefully over the heads of other parents, equally anxious, seated in rows of ballroom chairs, and play what had been practiced endlessly in preparation for the event.

In my case, it was the March from *Aida*. I remember an involuntary indrawn hiss (was it Father's?) as I went wrong toward the final chords.

The lessons (and the recitals) stopped after I went away to school because it turned out I was unable to read music, even the simplest notations. Assigned Debussy's *Bells*, the music teacher would remark on my playing the piece for him, "Well, that's sort of nice but it isn't *Bells*."

So I took to improvising pieces on the piano, just fooling around. After many years of this, my friends would remark how much the efforts sounded like the background music to such soap operas as *The Edge of Night*. It never occurred to me (or anyone else) that anything of this sort would ever get any kind of public performance, much less by a full-scale orchestra in a great concert hall.

To my surprise, it happened.

The circumstances were this. At a party, Cy Coleman, the Broadway composer (Will Rogers' *Follies*, *Life*, among others), heard me play a little waltz melody (less than a minute in length); he took my place at the piano and replayed the melody in a series of different rhythms—tangos, rumbas—and added some additional flourishes from classical and contemporary music, much to the amusement of the guests. At a birthday of mine he played it again; it was recorded on tape.

The organizing committee of my Harvard Fiftieth Anniversary felt it would be an interesting *amuse* (as the French call it) to have it included as part of the traditional Boston Pops salute to the Fiftieth class. What Cy Coleman had played was orchestrated by a friend, Bob Johnson, the director of the New York Philomusica Chamber Music Ensemble.

So that was why I found myself in Symphony Hall, moving stage front to tell the audience, many of them my classmates, about my waltz. T. S. Eliot once told someone that when he gave a poetry reading he felt like it was a kind of indecent exposure. I understood what he was talking about. I was carrying a triangle. The score of my waltz called for me to hit it twice. The Pops' conductor, Keith Lockhart, thought it appropriate that I should play the instrument.

I began by giving a short dissertation on the triangle. I told them how maligned it had been over the years, in particular by critics who felt that it had been overused in Franz Liszt's First Piano Concerto. I said this petulantly, as if I were a Liszt apologist. The audience stirred uneasily.

I went on to say that there were three particularly frightening things that could beset the triangle player—
l) that the triangle would spin sideways from its holding device so that the player, staring at the conductor for the cue, would miss it entirely;
2) that the triangle player, triangle held aloft, would look around for the stick (or rod) to hit it with and find it missing; and 3) (perhaps the most dismaying) that he would pick up the stick and find that the triangle itself was missing.

Then I talked briefly on the provenance of my waltz. I turned to Mr. Lockhart. He nodded and raised his baton.

My first sensation was one of enormous pride—to hear those familiar strains of my own making, however simple, first from the oboe, the flute and then flowing forth from the violin section, repeated in volume by the brass. I stood basking in it.

My pleasure was short-lived. I knew my entrance with the triangle was coming up. One of the terrors of orchestral music, of course, is that once it starts, there is no way it can be stopped. It's not like sports, where asking for a time-out is a constant. With music there's no way one can say, Hey, wait a minute, I'm not ready, I don't know where we are, and so on... One is borne inexorably up toward the moment of commitment. I was standing slightly in front of Mr. Lockhart, facing out toward the audience, so that I wasn't able to see him for any cue he might have given me. I was on my own. I held up the triangle, the stick poised, thinking my entrance was near, and then, realizing I was far too early, dropped it down. I could hear the laughter in the audience.

We reached a passage in the work, a slight solo piano part, which preceded my entrance. I raised the triangle again and, grimacing slightly, popped the stick against it. A bell-like tone drifted out over the audience. The piano solo was still being played, and I realized instantly that I'd come in a few measures too early. Idiotically, I tried to compensate for my mistake by hitting the triangle again. This time I hit it with my thumb, producing a dull thunk, as if I'd hit a lead pipe.

I lowered the triangle, appalled, staring bleakly out at the audience.

At the conclusion of the waltz I came in once again with the triangle—a climactic flourish from every instrument in the orchestra, my own among them, and this time I hit it on the button. There was applause, of course, and afterwards a lot of back-slapping from my classmates, but always that night the wrenching memory of the mis-hit.

Subsequently, I've often thought back on that moment—to have reached the crest, this sublime condition of having one's own work played by a great orchestra, and then self-destructing because of this egregious error, a leaden sound I can still hear in my head: Thunk!

Thinking back on the experience, I occasionally comfort myself with the knowledge that the orchestral score sits somewhere in the Boston Pops' archives, portfolio #365 or whatever. How pleasing to think that one evening its sheets may be spread out on the music stands. The program will read: Waltz. George Plimpton Opus 1. The triangle will be in the hands of a professional. I hope I have a friend there to tell me about it.

It was Fiedler, of course, who introduced the Boston Pops to the nation on *Evening at Pops*. Since 1969, this program has brought the excitement of the Boston Pops and the uniqueness of Symphony Hall to viewers around the country. It was through this series that the genre of American pops music was introduced to the American public. Many musical legends appeared in Symphony Hall with the Pops on this program. Among the guests during Fiedler's time were Ella Fitzgerald, Benny Goodman, Dave Brubeck, Dizzy Gillespie, Roberta Flack, Tony Bennett, Ethel Merman, Julia Child, and Sarah Vaughan. John Williams, beginning in 1980, brought his Hollywood panache and connections to the shows; his guests ranged from Ray Charles, Marilyn Horne,

Behind the scenes at a WGBH-TV taping of Evening at Pops *in the 1960s*

Edward M. Kennedy
A Family Tradition Continues

Senator Edward Kennedy narrating Copland's Lincoln Portrait *with Arthur Fiedler conducting the Boston Pops on* Evening at Pops, *1970*

My mother studied piano as a young woman at the New England Conservatory. She shared her love of music with our whole family and inspired us all with a lifelong love of music. Evenings at home often involved songs around the piano, with Mother leading us on and encouraging everyone to participate.

Mother always had a special place in her heart for Symphony Hall. Like generations of Bostonians, Friday afternoons she reserved for performances by her favorite orchestra. She

often took us to Saturday Children's Concerts, and we, too, came to appreciate the beauty and the acoustics of her beloved hall.

In addition to Symphony performances, the Pops Christmas concerts were another treasured Kennedy family tradition. The hall, decorated with loving care, was an unforgettable place to hear our favorite holiday carols.

Today, these cherished musical traditions live on. I now celebrate the holidays with my own children at

Symphony Hall and know that, before long, their children will also be singing with full hearts and creating new family memories that will endure through the years.

For a century, Symphony Hall has been a magnificent Boston landmark. Its brilliant presentations have become part of the nation's artistic heritage. It is also a symbol of shared memories, not just of music, but of wonderful times spent together with family and friends.

Symphony Hall decorated for Evening at Pops

Peter, Paul and Mary, and Jessye Norman to Yo-Yo Ma, Wynton Marsalis, and Itzhak Perlman. A sampler of *Evening at Pops* favorites during the Williams tenure would include the Richard Rodgers show in 1980, Broadway Night in 1982 (featuring Bernadette Peters), and a program showcasing the singing and dancing talent of Gregory Hines, in 1983.

Most recently, Keith Lockhart has brought a unique perspective to the show, thanks to his interest in creating programs with broader audience "pop culture" appeal—performers like k.d. lang, Allison Krauss, Bela Fleck, Penn & Teller, and Sarah Jessica Parker. He has also shown a great respect for traditional Pops connections, including Broadway artists such as Nathan Lane, Audra McDonald, Elaine Paige, Michael Feinstein, and Mandy Patinkin; and classical artists Gil Shaham, Dawn Upshaw, and Helen Huang. In addition, Lockhart has moved beyond the traditional Pops repertoire, with dance elements—Mark Morris, Forever Tango, Teatro Flamenco, and tap artists Bakari Wilder and Jimmy Slide—and strongly thematic programming—*A Copland Celebration*, *Brush Up Your Shakespeare*, and *The American Spirit*.

During Arthur Fiedler's time with the Pops, millions of Americans owned a least one of the hundreds of Boston Pops recordings. As might be expected, Symphony Hall was the "studio" for these recordings. At one marathon recording session, in July of 1935, forty pieces of music were recorded during a heat wave; to cope with the high temperatures, the orchestra (all men) played much of the music in various states of disrobement.

Symphony Hall is still favored for Pops recordings, since its sound is far superior to that of a conventional studio. Steven Spielberg, who has used the hall for recording two of his movie soundtracks said, "I think today that Symphony Hall is an instrument. Acoustically, it's a member of the orchestra." John Williams, renowned film composer and Pops conductor for fifteen years—

At right, celebrating with the Boston Pops at Symphony Hall; below, the installation of the Boston Pops sign on the roof of Symphony Hall—the true symbol of spring in Boston

EVENING AT POPS: THE PIERCE COLLECTION

For many of the 49 years that the Boston Symphony and Boston Pops have been broadcast on public radio, William Pierce (1920-1997) was the "voice" that accompanied these performances. In addition, he was an accomplished photographer who, when he wasn't capturing a performance for the airwaves, was capturing the Pops on film—the celebrities, sets, audience, and excitement that make up the Pops experience.

Julia Child

If Music Be the Food of Love

I'm not a musician. I did piano as a child, and it was clear I was not a piano player. I studied from the age of five on through high school. I made lots of noise, but I had no talent whatsoever. We've always had a piano, and I still pound around on it a little bit. I love Beethoven and Mozart and so forth. I always do the classics—in a terrible way!

My most intimate connection with Symphony Hall was when I did "Tubby the Tuba." It was in the sixties with Arthur Fiedler. I don't know how they happened to ask me. I guess they just wanted something new and different. I very much

enjoyed working with him. He was a real musician. I remember there was one passage in it when there was "four against three" or "three against four" which we practiced. I did it right during rehearsal, but when the actual thing came, I did it wrong. Nobody noticed it. But he did, of course, and I did. But I had a wonderful time.

I was mainly fascinated with Fiedler. He had great eyebrows. He had a perfect personality; nobody could copy that at all. Years later, when the Pops was on the Cape, in Hyannis, I had to lead the band in "Stars and Stripes Forever" with a jumbo wooden spoon.

We first moved to Cambridge in the late fifties; the Symphony played in Cambridge on occasion. Almost as soon as we got there, we subscribed for our seats. We attended Symphony, but not the Pops. We had seats next to nice people—in the middle, I think, in row T or U. It was wonderful, and I loved going. It was just a very pleasant experience. We dressed nicely—I wore my best bib!

and currently laureate conductor—made his mark on the organization by recording his popular film music with the Boston Pops in Symphony Hall. Moreover, he revived the importance of orchestras in film music. During his leadership, Williams continued the Pops legacy as the most frequently recorded orchestra in the world, with thirty albums to his credit. His successor, Keith Lockhart, has also brought a unique artistic vision to his Pops recordings. He has revitalized some of the music once recorded by Fiedler and Williams—swing, Gershwin, and some Holiday favorites—as well as commissioned new works. What's more, he has expanded the Pops repertoire by infusing world music: Celtic and Latin music were both included in recent recordings. In his first five years as Pops conductor—from 1995 to 2000—Lockhart made seven recordings.

Lockhart has also brought another dynamic to the Pops—an extraordinary commitment to connection with the audience, buoyed by respect for the traditions established by his predecessors. In Lockhart's opinion:

Symphony Hall is an integral partner in connecting with our audience. First, there is the sonic connection; the sound in Symphony Hall is so vibrant, so immediate, that the audience can actually feel *the music in a visceral way. When there is a big chord from the orchestra, it hits you physically—you can feel the vibration. This feeling makes an amazing difference in people's appreciation of live performance. Symphony Hall's intimacy is another important part of the formula. Even though the hall is rather large, when I address the audience, I can see the faces of the people I'm talking to. In Symphony Hall, the audience is not just a passive spectator; it* is *part of the performance.*

Throughout its history, Symphony Hall has been fundamental to the success of the Boston Pops. In turn, the Boston Pops and the pops musical genre itself continue to play an integral part in the history of Symphony Hall. Each year the Boston Pops performs more than ninety times in Symphony Hall and records six new television shows.

In sum, the legacies of the Boston Pops and Symphony Hall are inextricably joined. ✑

At left, Keith Lockhart and the Boston Pops; below left, Julia Child narrating Tubby the Tuba *for Evening at Pops in 1971, Arthur Fiedler conducting; below, the announcement of an encore: Cole Porter's "Night and Day"*

If Symphony Hall were a French food, it would be something hearty, like a great beef dish. A very fine Beef Bourgignon with a lovely sauce. Or it could be a roast loin strip with a Madeira sauce, Potatoes Anna, and asparagus tips.

Yes, Symphony Hall: serious and hearty!

REFLECTIONS

When a building is a great instrument for sound, our eyes go seeking the contours of that greatness. Half-consciously, idly, I look for visible signs of what makes a home for musical sounds, in the masses and surfaces of wood, plaster, wool, glass, brick, copper, brass, and stone. Niches, plinths, statuary, railings. The tons of material, worked by countless artisans, craftsmen, and laborers, so many cubic feet on Huntington Avenue, tuned and mellowed by time—all not inert, but an instrument. Not parts, but an organism. Visible, but with its work invisible. The mysterious current that runs between what we see and what we hear: ineluctable, elusive, teasing us out of thought, it is like the relationship—maybe it is an example of the relationship—between matter and spirit.

—*Robert Pinsky*

Patrons arriving at Symphony in the 1960s

Patrons waiting to make the mad dash for
seats at an open rehearsal

It has always been my belief that a city's greatness is judged by its symphony orchestra,
which gives the city a collection of dedicated
and educated musicians who disseminate spiritual values to the community.

   While the world knows of the rich historical significance of the centuries of the city
of Boston, the one hundred years of Symphony
Hall prove that Boston has the physical envi-
ronment so necessary to inspire, educate, and
refine its citizens.

   The building's unique quality makes it
a treasured musical landmark for which all of
us who deeply love and reverently cherish classical music will forever be indebted to Boston.

   My personal affection for Symphony
Hall is founded on the joy of the wonderful
acoustics, the thrilling audiences, but particularly the incredible musicians of the great
Boston Symphony Orchestra with its world-
renowned conductors—Charles Munch, Erich
Leinsdorf, and Seiji Ozawa.

   There can be no greater tribute to the
fine citizens of Boston than that they had the
cultivated vision and desire to build the world-
famous Symphony Hall.

   —VAN CLIBURN

Boston holds more than its share of exalting
civic spaces, and Symphony Hall, where so
many of us have rustled breathlessly into our
seats with not a moment to spare, is surely one
of them. Happy Birthday, grand old music
room!

   —JOHN UPDIKE

I've been all over Europe, and heard a lot
of the great orchestras in all of the great
halls. But, to me, Symphony Hall is the
most beautiful.

   At Symphony Hall, I walk onstage
and I pinch myself: I'm going out there, in this
beautiful hall, with the greatest orchestra in
the world. As I walk, this huge, gorgeous
orchestra creates a wave of sound behind me,
like a wind blowing me out into the audience,
the sound coming right over me and through
me. It's an incredible feeling, one of the best
I've ever had in my life—being on the front of
the stage, with this great audience from my
hometown, buoyed by the sound, the feeling in
my ears, of this orchestra, all ninety or so
members. The acoustics are fabulous.

   I began my association with the
Boston Pops in Washington in the late 1960s
with Arthur Fiedler, narrating Prokofiev's Peter
and the Wolf. Fiedler was the one who taught
me the protocol of how to take my bows. In
the 1980s I worked with John Williams in
Benjamin Britten's Young Person's Guide to
the Orchestra. Over the years, I've worked
with the Pops on tours in Bonn, Germany, on
the Esplanade, at Tanglewood, and in
Symphony Hall.

Anticipating opening night in front of
Symphony Hall, 1999

My boyfriend had been a subscriber to the
Symphony for many years before we met. He
introduced me to the magic of Symphony during the months of our courtship. He took me to
my first opening night on September 25, 1996.
We enjoyed champagne and hors d'oeuvres
while mingling in our black-tie attire. Minutes
before the concert was to begin, my boyfriend
pulled me aside and asked, "Are you free for
the next fifty or so opening nights?" As he
spoke he pulled a small jewelry box out of his
tuxedo pocket. "Because I'd like you to marry
me." The tears welled in my eyes, and, of
course, I said yes. Now, a few years later, we
continue to celebrate this special memory at
Symphony Hall. My husband and I look forward to spending at least forty-seven more
opening nights at the BSO.

   —ELISA MARKS

I've delighted in being an audience
member as well. I went to concerts in Symphony
Hall until 1963, when Senator Kennedy and I
moved to Washington for twenty years. When I
returned to Boston in the early 1980s, I subscribed to the symphony. I had fabulous seats on
the floor, in the middle of the hall. After a year,
I changed to the left balcony overlooking the
stage, where you're sitting right over the soloist
and can see the conductor up close. You see the
whole orchestra—the brass, the woodwinds, the
percussion—instead of just the strings. And you
can see backstage when they open the doors for
the soloists and the conductor. It's wonderfully
exciting.

   To this day, I bring a lot of new people
to Symphony Hall. I'm able to teach them about
the orchestra, pointing out the different sections
from my perch in the balcony. Symphony Hall
seems like a temple, but it isn't solemn. I bring
guests first to the Pops, telling them, "This can
be fun, you'll have a wonderful evening, bring
your children!" A lot have since become subscribers.

   I will never tire of introducing people to
this beautiful hall and this wonderful orchestra.

   —JOAN KENNEDY

Wartime sign posted on Symphony Hall;
Koussevitzky supported many patriotic efforts.

Symphony Hall has given much, heard much,
and holds many secrets. Every generation tells
a different tale.

   We college students of the late fifties,
in our center-balcony rush seats, were overcome by the sheer sound. Was there also a
building? Seats, doors? The students I sent
over in the eighties, eyewitnesses, gave an
architectural report—the genteel symmetrical
formality, the organ pipes, the churchlike pews.

   Future generations will need it more
than ever, when the best unrecorded, unampli-
fied sound will be imbibed like rare nectar.
Symphony Hall's simple geometry will refresh
like an indoor version of our greatest national
parks.

   —JOHN HARBISON

Ladies enjoying Pops punch

Centuries ago, only royalty and aristocrats were permitted to attend performances of the works of the masters. This select group would rattle their jewelry in approval of Bach's Concerto in D minor or at the climax of Beethoven's Fifth.

Back in the unimaginable era when television and the Internet did not exist, concert halls served as meeting places, providing townspeople with a sense of culture and community. Throughout history, music has been the great communicator and community builder.

Thanks to Symphony Hall, we Bostonians and New Englanders can enjoy those very same performances today that were once reserved for the fashionable few. For the last hundred years, this concert hall—so rich in tradition—has brought us the greatest musicians in the world. Only at Symphony Hall can we see so many diverse artists in one place. On the same stage where Handel's Messiah is performed, we can also hear the classic American folk music of Arlo Guthrie or the hometown hilarity of Steve Sweeney.

My fondest memory of Symphony Hall is that unforgettable evening when I performed with the Boston Pops. Later that same night, I had the great privilege of introducing my father—a Juilliard-trained pianist and my earliest musical influence—to John Williams.

From Fiedler to Ozawa, from Dickson to Lockhart, Symphony Hall has been, and will continue to be, Boston's cultural time capsule. Perhaps the rattling of jewelry has faded with the years, but the energy and passion of the music remain.

—STEVEN TYLER

Among the first items to attend to after I was admitted to Tufts Medical School in 1956 was obtaining a subscription to the Boston Symphony Orchestra. I had been attending the BSO series in Providence for years while in high school and in college.

Accordingly, I presented myself in person at the Symphony Hall subscription office. There I met the manager of subscriptions, a motherly woman whose name now escapes me. Together we reviewed what seats might be available for Saturday nights. The rigors of medical school both precluded any other series and demanded the spiritual restoration to be provided on Saturday evenings. In those days, no desirable seats were available. There were, however, two seats in the orchestra in the center, a few rows behind the break. The problem was that the seats, though in the same row, were not together: there were three seats between them. Since the seats were just about in the center, the subscription director saw no reason why the folks in those three seats would not be willing to move in one direction or the other if I would ask. I took her advice and purchased the two seats.

It is important to know that I came to Boston quite unattached and depended on the kindness of friends and chance to meet young women to accompany me on Saturday nights. On that first concert of the season (all Beethoven, as I recall), I asked the young couple occupying two of the three intervening seats if they would mind moving one way or the other. They gladly agreed. Sitting in the third seat, however, was a woman of advanced and indeterminate age. She had been occupying that particular seat for an advanced and equally indeterminate number of years. That seat was at the point where the section seats joined. (At that junction there are two arms between seats rather than one.) She stated in a very determined and optimistic manner that she was going to occupy that seat far into the future. The stated reason was the extra armrest, but I expect that even without that extra comfort the answer would have been no different.

So for the remainder of that entire season I took a series of young ladies to Symphony every Saturday night. To each I explained that we would not be sitting together. That explanation was taken with varying degrees of grace. Few, if any, for various reasons, were asked back. In some cases I actually found it an advantage to be seated separately. Also, I did become friends with the lady in the seat with the extra arm. Whatever the quality of my companions (usually first dates), the conversation with the lady was always cordial and pleasant.

When the time for renewal arrived, I again presented myself to the director of subscriptions and told her of the events related to those two seats. She apparently took pity on this poor medical student and magically produced two seats in Row A in the first balcony—next to each other!

Since that time, many things have changed. I married. Children appeared and grew up. On occasion they shared the seats. Contrary to expectations, I divorced and remarried and started a practice in Providence. Through all the changes and intermittent turmoil one constant remained: the Saturday concerts. The seats have moved and are now a little closer to the stage—still Row A, first balcony. My wife and I continue to share them and the pleasures of the music.

For over 40 years in Symphony Hall I have had light shed upon darkness, felt releases from the stresses of life, and obtained repeated spiritual renewal. Thanks to the BSO, to Symphony Hall, and to the kind woman who bestowed the seats on me so many years ago.

—HERBERT RAKATANSKY, M.D.

A sold-out house for a rehearsal, 1999

Caroline Smedvig
Pictures from an Institution

I work in a third-floor walk-up. My comrades include a truculent pigeon who frequents the sill of my lone window and a tribe of mice.

Welcome to a Symphony Hall known only by a few. This landscape, like most things about Symphony Hall, was shaped by our founding father, Major Higginson, who cared not a whit for "office space." All he needed to run an orchestra, he said, was a desk (he did accede to a small box office). Since room for the hundred-plus staff was never part of the original blueprint, the past hundred years have seen the exploitation and annexation of every square inch, from the bowels of the boiler room to my own garret digs.

Like early Christians in the catacombs, we abide where we can. For some, this means in retrofitted ventilation systems, cold storage, and reconstructed air shafts. This scarcity triggers a rush to stake your claim first, ask questions later. More than one "space planner"—in the parlance of the late twentieth century—has examined the warren of offices and run screaming into the Fens.

It's an upstairs-downstairs existence. The public rubs elbows with the gilded cherub and the marble staircase while we live with pipe staging and temperamental plumbing. Take Higginson's, and his architect Charles McKim's, handling of the brick. The facades of the building that face Massachusetts and Huntington avenues were built with a rosy-hued glazed brick of the highest quality. On the southwest facade, facing St. Stephen's Street, the brick changes to an industrial warehouse quality—durable, but noticeably inferior. This is the side where the orchestra and staff enter through the stage door—unmarked and unheralded, save by a discreet burgundy awning.

I have walked the route from this entrance to my office for more than twenty years. From the first flight of stairs, you are Oedipus at the crossroads: Proceed straight and you enter the realm of the crimson carpets; hang a right and you're home with the orchestra, the stage crew, the staff, the insiders of all stripes.

Before each concert, this narrow inlet that connects stage right and left is the province of the artists. One hundred musicians warm up, adjust a tie, a reed, a string. Carrying their instruments like Roman shields in front of them, cellists jostle to make their way. The intonement of "five minutes, onstage please," increases the tension. Visiting agents, record company executives, and garden variety hangers-on circle one another in an uneasy dance of the cranes.

I find this part of the hall at its best early or late in the day, in the interstices between rehearsals and performance. In that congested hallway, the green velvet berths that house the cellos are empty now. They face whatever spillover of percussion that the week's program might dictate strewn along the opposite wall. The light from St. Stephen's Street filters through the opalescent skin of the bass drum. There are almost always xylophones, snares, the occasional Chinese gong, a bell tree, and tam-tam. Sometimes Vic Firth's timpani are even tucked away there, their wooden covers the perfect resting place for a handbag or cappuccino. Reading material, like *Popular Mechanics* and *International Dredging Review*, is stacked on the radiators, next to the basket of earplugs for Pops season or Mahler. Then you face a stairway leading past the men's and ladies' dressing rooms, where the onstage finery of the orchestra members is stashed in high school gym lockers. Keep climbing, and you'll see closed doors that lead to the radio booths and their secret, one-way windows covered with black theatrical scrim. While invisible to the audience, they afford the announcer a perch from which to view the events onstage and allow the play-by-play commentary made famous by the late William Pierce (once the subject of a *New Yorker* cartoon). The final stairway is not for the faint of heart. At the summit, you pick your way through black coils of cable and Super Trooper spotlights—the *Evening at Pops* lighting burial ground—and only then will you have arrived at the press office (prompting more than one member of the fourth estate to remark: "You sure don't make it easy").

Little about working in Symphony Hall is easy. Even a soloist must choose between the freight elevator and nothing. Only in 1987 was the elevator modernized, from a water-operated contraption requiring fifty-five gallons for the ride up, which was then flushed for the ride down. The inner sanctum of the Music Director's dressing room has boasted the same plumbing for five decades. Time here is measured not in years but reigns, as in, "That's a Leinsdorf toilet."

Symphony Hall has its seasons, too. In September, there is the "back to school" feel with the return of the Tanglewood émigrés. There is always a fresh coat of polyurethane on the hardwood floors and freshly painted stage door stairs with the white lip on the battleship gray treads, which will have already faded by the first frost. One day in December, red apples mysteriously appear, suspended from every chandelier, which will pass for Christmas decor. After New Year's, the hall is infused with the scent of curried goat when the orchestra's stage manager, Cleve Morrison, prepares the Jamaican specialty in an annual tradition.

One of the great miracles of this building is its perennial ability to reinvent itself. Every spring the sober, straight-backed chairs literally disappear through a giant hole in the floor via a concealed elevator—and *voilà*, it's Pops season. Only in Boston could tiny, formica-topped tables surrounded by five (not four or six) neon-green chairs pass muster. The hall seems to shrug its shoulders at the time-honored decorative alterations it must endure.

Symphony Hall is a survivor. It has made it through world wars, hurricanes, floods, bad furniture, a pyromaniac, and e-mail. And it has done so with a patrician grace, its own kind of noblesse oblige.

Each time I fling open a door to the second balcony—a matter of feet from my office—and enter the hall itself, nothing else matters. It is that rare sacred space with its living memory, a constant refuge from the world and its claims, at any hour, for any generation. As Yeats said:

We are blest by everything,
Everything we look upon is blest.

View through the leather-clad doors across the second balcony

CONTRIBUTORS

SAM ALLIS (*The Sitting Experience*) is a writer for the *Boston Globe*.

R.W. APPLE JR. (*The Real Thing*) is the chief correspondent of the *New York Times*.

DR. LEO BERANEK (*The Acoustics of Symphony Hall*), a lifetime trustee of the Boston Symphony, is recognized internationally as an authority in the field of sound and acoustics. A recipient of the Acoustical Society of America's Wallace C. Sabine Medal and its Gold Medal, he has consulted on the acoustical design of dozens of halls around the world.

PAUL SPENCER BYARD (*The Genius of Symphony Hall: A Legacy for the Future*) is a New York architect and the Director of the Columbia University Historic Preservation Program. Paul Spencer Byard and his firm, Platt Byard Dovell Architects, are collaborating with Anne Beha Associates in the Symphony Hall Master Plan update. Mr. Byard directed the preparation of the 1985 Master Plan and the conceptual design that became Ozawa Hall.

ROBERT CAMPBELL (*Bricks and Mortar: The Design of Symphony Hall*) is an architect and writer in Cambridge, Massachusetts and the architecture critic of the *Boston Globe*.

JULIA CHILD (*If Music Be the Food of Love*) is known to millions as the chef who brought gourmet cooking to public television. She is the author of many best-sellling cookbooks, including *The Way to Cook*, *The French Chef Cookbook*, and the forthcoming *Julia's Kitchen Wisdom: Essential Techniques and Recipes from a Lifetime of Cooking*, to be published in November 2000.

VAN CLIBURN has enjoyed a near-legendary reputation since winning the 1958 Tchaikovsky International Piano Competition in Moscow. He continues to perform frequently and maintains a strong philanthropic interest in the arts and arts education.

AARON COPLAND (*Portrait of a Symphony: 1960 & 2000*) is regarded as the dean of American composers. His association with the BSO dates to 1925 with the premiere of his *Music for the Theatre*. He went on to become one of the most often commissioned and performed American composers.

HARRY ELLIS DICKSON (*Memories of Youth*), Associate Laureate Conductor of the Boston Pops, is the founder of the Boston Symphony Youth Concerts.

EVERETT FIRTH (*A View from the Stage*) is the timpanist of the Boston Symphony Orchestra.

CHARLES GAUTHIER (*Metamorphosis*) is a photographer living in Boston. He is currently working on a book on American popular culture.

STEPHEN JAY GOULD (*The Soul of a City*) is Agassiz Professor of Zoology at Harvard University and a lifelong choral singer.

JOHN HARBISON is an eminent American composer living in Cambridge, Massachusetts. Among his many honors have been the Pulitzer Prize and the Metropolitan Opera's commission of his opera, "The Great Gatsby."

EDWARD M. KENNEDY (*A Family Tradition Continues*) is the senior United States Senator from Massachusetts.

JOAN KENNEDY is a philanthropist, supporter of the arts, and author of *The Joy of Classical Music: A Guide for You and Your Family*.

STEVEN LEDBETTER (*Under the Sign of Beethoven*) was Musicologist and Program Annotator of the Boston Symphony Orchestra from 1979 to 1998. Among his specialties is Boston's musical history in the late nineteenth and early twentieth centuries.

KEITH LOCKHART (*The Next Generation* and "*America's Orchestra*") is the Conductor of the Boston Pops and the Music Director of the Utah Symphony Orchestra.

YO-YO MA (*Introduction*) is a cellist who frequently performs with the Boston Symphony Orchestra.

CONSTANTINE MANOS (*Portrait of a Symphony: 1960 & 2000*) was first commissioned to photograph the Boston Symphony Orchestra in 1960, at age 19. He is the author of five books and a member of Magnum Photos.

ELISA MARKS is a resident of Boston and has attended BSO performances since 1996.

SEIJI OZAWA (*First Impressions*) is Music Director of the Boston Symphony Orchestra through the 2002 season; he will then become Music Director of the Vienna State Opera.

WILLIAM PIERCE (Evening at Pops: *The Pierce Collection*) was the host of the Boston Symphony and Boston Pops broadcasts on WGBH public radio for more than 40 years. He was also an amateur photographer who chronicled many Pops performances.

ROBERT PINSKY, Professor of English and Creative Writing at Boston University, served as United States Poet Laureate from 1997-2000.

GEORGE PLIMPTON (*Opus 1*) is the editor of *Paris Review*. Among his many books are *Out of My League*, *Paper Lion*, *The Curious Case of Sidd Finch*, and, most recently, *Pet Peeves, or Whatever Happened to Doctor Rawff?*, published in 2000.

HERBERT RAKATANSKY, M.D. resides in Providence, Rhode Island and has subscribed to the BSO since 1956.

JOHN ROCKWELL (*I Was a Teenage Program-Passer*) writes for the *New York Times*.

CAROLINE SMEDVIG (*Casts of Character: The Symphony Statues* and *Pictures from an Institution*) has worked under the sign of Beethoven for twenty years.

STEVEN SPIELBERG (*Rolling*) is a film director.

STEVEN TYLER is a songwriter and the lead singer of the band Aerosmith.

JOHN UPDIKE is the author of fifty-one books, including *Golf Dreams: Writings on Golf*. His most recent novel is *Gertrude and Claudius*.

PETER VANDERWARKER (photographs of architectural details) is the co-author (with Robert Campbell) of *Cityscapes of Boston*. His current book, *The Big Dig: Reshaping an American City*, will be published by Little, Brown in 2001.

JOHN WILLIAMS (*Symphony Hall in the Dark* and *The Story of My Grandfather's Hammer*) is a leading film composer and is Laureate Conductor of the Boston Pops.

SUSAN WILSON (*As the Century Turned: Boston in 1900*) is an author and photographer whose work regularly appeared in the *Boston Globe* from 1978 to 1996. Her books include *Boston Sites and Insights*, *Garden of Memories*, and *Literary Trail of Greater Boston*.